MW01538574

NORTH
OF THE
SOO

WILDERNESS ADVENTURE STORIES

JOHN H. GEAREY

NORTH OF THE SOO
Copyright © 2014, John Gearey

ISBN: 978-1-4600-0329-9
LSI Edition: 978-1-4600-0330-5
E-book ISBN: 978-1-4600-0331-2
(E-book available from the Kindle Store, KOBO and the iBooks Store)

Cataloguing data available from Library and Archives Canada

Dedicated to the memory of my good friend Cris Huizing,
explorer, hunter and outdoor enthusiast.

Contents

Introduction

As the days of our lives slip away we retain the memories of times long past that thrilled us and swept us into adventure and fun. Someone once said adventure is only another word for trouble. As we look back to those times of excitement and challenge in our younger years I must admit there is a lot of truth to that saying.

Within the pages of this book you will find several stories of both excitement and trouble experienced mainly in the wilds of Northern Ontario in the area of Algoma, north of Sault Ste. Marie, along with a story from the Porcupine Mountain area in Northern Michigan and one other that took place in New Brunswick and Ontario.

All the accounts written here are based on true events but with some name changes and some literary license used to fill in where my memory was weak. For those who are in these stories I ask forgiveness if they recall some of the events differently.

It is my sincere hope you will enjoy your read of mishap, adventure and fun.

John Gearey
Feb. 2014

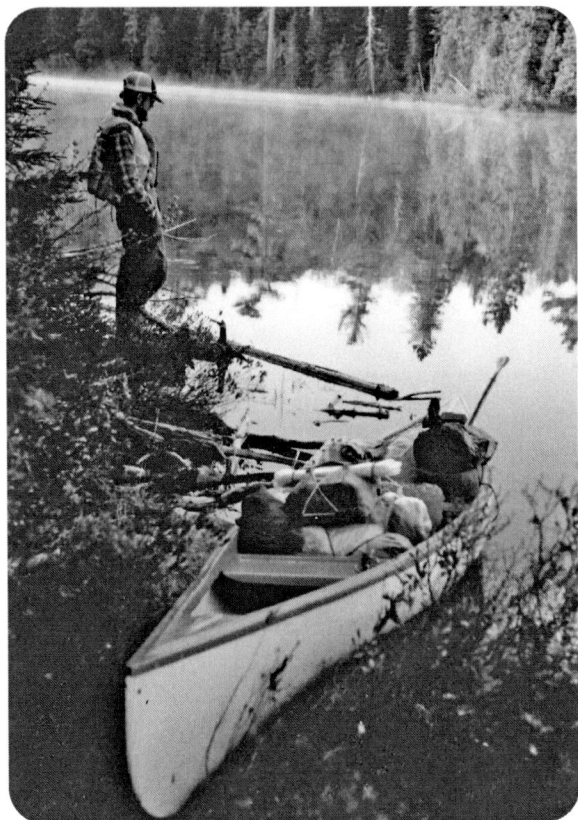

The author

A Winter Camping Miracle

The day was cold. The kind of cold that pervades your bones. The kind that makes you wish you'd stayed within the warm walls of your home. However the thrill of adventure and the hope of good fishing brought a group of us to a remote and frozen lake a little south of a small community called Batchawana Bay.

We had arrived at Tilley Lake. Frozen to a depth we could only guess, we stared at the snow covered expanse that stretched flat and bleak for a mile before us. Tim Nott and I had planned this trip with seven teenage boys who belonged to the Christian Service Brigade from our local church. An organization formed as an alternate to the Boy Scouts of America with additional emphasis on faith in Jesus. Thus here we stood on this sunny, frosty Saturday morning with our toboggans loaded with camping gear that included sleeping bags, pads, tents and all kinds of paraphernalia we thought would be needed.

Bundled up in heavy jackets, boots and mitts we strapped on our snowshoes. The boys had their packsacks filled with fishing gear, snacks, drinks and who knows what else they had put together the night before.

Leaving the trucks we headed through the trees and out unto the lake looking for a suitable place to set up camp for the next couple of days. The boys were full of excitement and anticipation and the cold air did not seem to bother them. However Tim and I knew what long days and nights in the extreme cold could mean if precaution was not observed. For now the young men were talking about fishing and making igloos from the snow on the lake and many other topics that I ignored.

At the moment finding dry firewood and lots of it was the most pressing need. We hiked down the lake shuffling through a foot of snow and in a short time had come upon a point of land that looked promising for a place to set up permanent camp. This area of the lake appeared to have a good drop off where fish might congregate and the shore had an abundance of dead conifers some still standing and others partially fallen. Several pine and spruce trees stood stark and bare through the surrounding bush which would help make a good starter fire and not far away stood a couple of dead hardwoods that would make for a longer lasting fire. We decided this was where we should stay.

Our first task was to stomp down a large area that would accommodate our tents, fire pit and fishing holes. The plan was to dig a pit just off the ice on the shoreline and then place the larger hardwoods on the bottom and pile the softwoods on top. As the boys began this task I took my axe and saw and headed for the nearby trees planning to cut up some of the dead spruce and pine that lay above the snow. I had spotted a couple of dead white birch just back in the bush a few yards that would work well for the base. Taking off my snowshoes in order to accommodate the process of cutting up the trees I soon found myself waist deep in the soft snow, axe in one hand, saw in the other floundering around like a beached whale in a sea of white fluff.

I grabbed the nearest branch of a fallen tree and tried to extricate a foot. However something had managed to grip my foot deep under the snow and would not release it. While I was tugging and straining to free myself I fell forward landing face first in a white soft drift. To my chagrin several of the boys saw my dilemma and loudly displayed their pleasure in the form of laughter and verbal comments of which I will not bore you or my return reply.

Presently a number of the boys began to help out by going along the shoreline and dragging the cut trees and branches back to the fire pit. For many of the boys their thoughts were on fishing so several of them were collecting alder gads and willow branches that grew along the shoreline while others were attempting to drill holes in the ice.

Initially there was a great frenzy of activity as the young men rushed to and fro in their eagerness to get a fire going or get to fishing. However it soon became apparent that for those attempting to drill through hard ice there are those who have more stamina and will power than others. Some had begun with great enthusiasm and zeal but in a short time their strength began to wane and with that so did their determination. And so for some they found they would rather play in the snow or stand around the fire than make a hole in the ice in order to catch a fish.

For others though the hard work seemed to inspire them and the dream of catching big fish was a great motivator. Tim and I watched as we set up tents and helped some to organize their equipment while keeping an eye on the fellows and their hole drilling. We knew certain precautions were necessary in the use of this device for safety reasons and for keeping the blades sharp. Often the blades are dulled by banging the auger on the ice when attempting to remove the slush or ice forming around the blades and we had no way to sharpen the edges.

After some hard work the holes finally were drilled and the bait, mostly live minnows were lowered down through the icy water all in the hopes of catching some unwary fish. The boys often came back to the campfire to warm up and roast their cold sandwiches and have a hot drink. We were all thankful for the sun as it reflected off the surface of the snow on the lake but were aware of the danger of the warming rays and the damage they can cause to your skin and eyes if caution is not observed. Although the sun was brilliant the cold air still went deep into the lungs and for some their noses turned white when they faced the wind for any length of time.

In the beginning our small band of outdoor enthusiasts had raced across the ice in eagerness and expectation but now with the moving of time came the slowly developing realization of a chill developing in the inner core brought on by exposure to the frigid air. Hands and feet were growing cold and many of the boys were becoming bored with fishing as there was a lack of activity from below the ice. The wonderment of the frozen lake was waning and some of them began to think how much warmer it would be at home and how much more fun it would be playing games or watching television.

The fire had proved to be a source of amusement at first for the fellows but as the day progressed they simply stood around the perimeter of the pit and watched the flames burn into the dry sticks they threw in. Often the snow would fall in and send showers of sparks and volumes of smoke high in the air.

Tim and I had spent some time in showing the boys how to hook their minnows and worms up properly and how to drop the bait down to within a foot or so off the bottom. As well we showed them how to jig their lures and how to attach their lines to the gads and secure them in a small pile of watered down snow beside the holes.

We had erected two main tents near the campfire and now were preparing for what would be a cold night. We hoped the boys sleeping bags would keep them warm enough. They needed a good nights rest so they could handle the rigors of the next day.

Two brothers who were the oldest of the group had headed around the nearest point and were no longer visible. They had taken an ax and saw and all their personal supplies and I wondered what they had in mind. Another boy who was younger had joined the brothers Ralph and Lloyd and as time passed my curiosity grew. I had been busy helping the rest of the gang set up the site and getting down to the task of fishing but finally I decided I must find out what was going on around the corner.

Over the years I have found many folks need time and space to work out their own ideas and plans. And so it was on this frosty morning that I had given the three boys a space of nearly two hours to themselves. I knew the brothers being sixteen and seventeen wanted to be independent but they were often on the verge of denying authority. However as a leader my responsibility was to keep the boys safe even if was from themselves so I went in search of them to find out what was going on.

As I rounded the corner I could see the framework of a large tepee. They had erected three trimmed pine poles, some fifteen feet tall with the butts stuck securely in the snow and the tops tied together with rope. The young men were in the process of wrapping what appeared to be a huge piece of canvas around the poles. In the clear air of the wilderness a voice rang out loud and clear. "Come on over Captain John and see our new home." Ralph the oldest boy and often the most rebellious was waving to me. Already in his young life he had managed to turn his parents hair prematurely grey and his father seemed to have less hair lately perhaps as some thought from pulling it out in bouts of frustration.

However I had an affinity for the boy as he often made me laugh. I recalled one Sunday morning he came and shook my hand at the church. Our Pastor had been ill that day and I had given the morning message. He thanked me and said how much he appreciated the sermon. This comment intrigued me coming from Ralph so I asked him why he liked it. I knew better but I asked anyhow. His answer was blunt and to the point "Cause Captain John, it was short and we're done by twelve o'clock." Thus once again I was reminded to never think too much of ones self because the young people of this world will quickly humble you with their openness and truthfulness.

Now I stood staring at this large tepee with the backdrop of the grey and white trees standing behind. At that moment I began to realize the importance of a leader staying in touch with all those in his care. Many thoughts began to invade my mind and all the possible ramifications of actions taken or not taken.

Let me explain. During the Nineteen Eighties the Canadian government had begun to realize how poorly we had exercised our privilege as custodians of the wilderness and the over-use of our renewable resources. We as a people in general had not given much thought to the usage of the forests and wildlife we had been blessed with in this country. For the past two hundred years we had done pretty much what we wished when it came to using the outdoors for commercial or individual use especially on Crown Lands. Here in the north most assumed it was our inherent right so we happily went about doing what we wished at the time. That was now in the process of changing. The Ministry of Natural Resources had brought in new regulations governing the usage of crown land for all activities including camping, fishing and hunting.

Knowing all this I now stood surveying the scene before me and realizing we were law breakers. The boys had cut three green pine trees and trimmed the branches so they could use them for uprights on the tepee. There was a new law in place that prohibited such actions and to compound this error the third boy was busy carrying out armloads of green boughs to be used for a mattress.

Conscious of my failure to inform and supervise properly I cast a furtive glance around expecting to see a Conservation Officer running across the lake or a helicopter hovering overhead commanding us to stand where we were and not move. I envisioned being given a lecture long on the rules in front of the group and then being handed a large fine. My embarrassment as a law breaker and ultimate disgrace as a youth leader flashed before my eyes. What was I to do?

As I approached the boys they had an excited look in their eyes and a desire to see approval from me. I knew I must be cautious with what I said and the way I handled the situation. Perhaps later at home in a meeting I would outline the new rules and my failure to tell them in advance. The youths could use the boughs as they had conveniently forgotten to bring any sort of foam pads to sleep on. As a responsible leader I should have taken the time to check each individual pack to be sure they had what they needed.

However at this moment I had few choices and I felt the harm had already been done. I simply told the fellows that in the future to be sure to let me know their plans before hand. What I did not know at that moment that it would not be long before the brothers would once again help me to grow in wisdom.

I hurried back to the main campsite to help Tim begin preparations for the evening supper meal and make sure things were ready for the night time. The suns reflecting rays on the glistening snow along with a tranquil wind helped create a serene setting for those huddled around the warm fire. Several of the group were in a state of relaxation as they sipped on hot chocolate seated in their sling chairs while watching the fishing lines for some movement.

Moments as these are often short lived. Suddenly one of the boys yelled "fish on." Everyone came alive. Chairs were tossed aside as the rush was on to see the first action of the day. Other lines were abandoned without thought as the boys ran to the hole with the stick that was jerking up and down violently. Joey a thirteen year old had grasped the slippery line and was struggling to bring the fish to the surface. All kinds of advice was flowing to encourage him. "Did you set the hook well?"

"Keep the pressure on, don't give the fish any slack."

"Watch the bottom of the hole so you don't cut your line on the ice."

Joey continued to bring up the fish hand over hand on the line but then he hesitated. A crucial moment had arrived. The line seemed to be caught. We give him advice to keep the line taunt as the finned one has come up against the bottom of the ice and the fish could be lost if not maneuvered into the hole carefully. Everyone held their breath as Joey continued to try to bring up the fish. He pulls hard and then suddenly out of the hole came a huge fish that landed in the nearby snow.

Disappointment can come in many different packages. Here was our hope that the fish on the ice before us would be a huge walleye, that great eating fish we all enjoy. But no! Wait a moment. That large hunk of fish lying there is not our beloved pickerel as we Canadians like to call them but an ugly grey hulk with fins despised by all fishermen. With those big fat pulsating lips it was none other than a whistle trout, that bottom hugging vermin of a fish called a SUCKER. Enough said. The disappointment was immediate and then most turn away while others help Joey take the hook out of the monstrous extended lips.

The excitement was over and we all went back to our holes to check the lines. Somehow the day seemed colder and bleaker than before. For many the thrill of catching fish was the reason they came while for others it was the challenge and fun of doing something in the outdoors. For now some of them began to build igloos and snow forts while others headed across the lake on snowshoes to explore an unusual appearing object. The raspy voice of a raven could be heard from a distant shoreline perhaps voicing his disapproval of the newcomers or telling his friends there was some food being left on the ice.

One of the favorite birds in the north is the Whisky Jack or properly called the Canadian Grey Jay a cousin of the Blue Jay but not as loud. They are very friendly and often come to pick up food around the campfire but can be a nuisance at times stealing food left unattended so some have nicknamed them "Camp Robbers." When sitting still these birds will sometimes come and sit on a shoulder or knee and take food from your hand thus they can be a welcome diversion in the silent world of winter in the north. Sadly for some unknown reason we had not been privileged with their presence to this point of time.

Tim and I had kept up a steady search for dry wood through the day. We kept cutting several kinds of dead trees and branches and the boys kept the fire burning and as well we had stock piled enough wood for the evening and morning fires.

Stew. Feeding seven hungry teenagers and two tired adults the easiest and best supper without question has to be stew unless of course you've been blessed with a catch of fresh fish. Stew can have a variety of ingredients that can taste good from chopped up beef, carrots, onions, potatoes along with an assortment of other things including but not limited to chunks of whistle trout, left over sandwiches, candy wrappers, apple cores, orange peels and whatever else the boys felt they needed to dispose of. All would taste good out here in the wilds when you are starved. Thankfully we had brought two large pots of stew prepared at home and we now put it all together in one very large pot to simmer over the fire while we sliced great slabs of Italian bread in huge quantities.

On days when the temperature struggles to achieve -20 C

it is well to remember to keep food thawed and near the fire if eating is important at all. Chocolate bars freeze solid. Soft drinks become popsicles in a can. Sandwiches become slabs of granite. Even hot drinks turn cold rapidly. These were some of the lessons the young people learned along with how quickly wet pant legs become frozen cloth from playing in the snow. Through out the day they found themselves rotating their chilled legs and backsides to the fire in a never ending attempt to keep warm.

The surrounding area near the fire pit was blackened from the smoke and burnt embers and was continuing collapsing from the heat. Everyone tried to be careful not to slide in or lose their balance but the hanging tea kettles were often upset and along with the toasting grills would often slide into the burning wood below. The evening meal did not take long to be over and now with the boys hunger abated all were looking forward to a large night fire and some tall stories of the wilderness.

Darkness comes early in January in the north once the sun drops behind a western hill and then the temperature drops quickly. Have you ever stood on the frozen surface of a northern lake at twilight and felt the frigid air move across the white expanse? Have you ever watched the sun set behind a barren hill and feel the deep cold of night with the whisper of death in the air? Have you ever felt the icy grip of winter creep into your bones and wonder if you'll ever feel truly warm again?

We threw another log on the fire and filled our mugs with hot drinks and huddled closer together. Time passed as the night grew colder and colder and very shortly the boys were heading for their beds and I prayed they would be warm enough through the night. The stars had come out in all their glory and the night air had become extremely sharp as I went about checking the tents. I found Lloyd sitting on a blanket outside his tepee. I asked him how things were. He motioned towards the door flap and said he was waiting for the smoke to clear. Evidently the smoke from their small fire on the inside had not funneled up through the air hole in the peak properly so he had come outside to take in some fresh air. I left the three fellows hoping they would leave the fire alone and go to bed.

Silence came gradually over our small band of adventurers as one by one the voices inside the tents trailed off. I crawled into my down sleeping bag feeling tired but comfortable. During the night I awoke and stuck my nose out of the bag. All was quiet and very cold but a strong urge to take a stroll on the ice came over me. I unzipped my bag and slid my feet to the floor and took a look out the tent door. The moon shone bright and I could see nearly as well as if it were daylight and all was still and tranquil as I stepped out of the tent. And then in the clear night air came a loud popping noise from somewhere down the lake. I stood and listened and the sound came again like a rifle shot from the direction of a nearby shore. What was that noise? Ah yes, it must be the frost penetrating the outer bark of a tree and invading the inner core causing all sorts of strange noises in the winter.

Standing there in the moonlight I felt a deep chill run through my body. I had stayed too long outside in only my long johns. I felt cold, far too cold and my whole body was shaking. I crawled back into the tent and into my bag.

Daylight came and offered a new beginning and a new hope of good fishing. I hurriedly dressed and went out to inspect the fire pit.

Most of the wood had burned over night so I began anew with cedar shavings and some birch bark we had saved. With the help of several small dead pine branches the fire was soon roaring and in a matter of minutes the boys had gathered around the pit eagerly awaiting the pancakes and sausages they had been promised.

The coffee was soon perking and Tim had thrown the sausages into a large frying pan when my thoughts turned to the trio around the corner. There had been no sound from that direction since we got up.

"Breakfast!" Tim yelled and within minutes we heard some loud shrieking coming from that direction and then we could see Ralph in his long johns running through the snow in his bare feet headed towards us. The sight will always remain etched in my memory. Then abruptly half way to the campfire while still yelling he turned and began to run back from where he had come.

There are few ways I can accurately describe what we had all just witnessed. To say he resembled a wounded deer in intense pain trying to flee in deep snow would only partially describe the event. With his knees jerking up to his chest as he ran agonizing from his feet making contact with the ice and snow along with his shrieking from the pain this indeed was something to witness. The other boys at the campfire had enjoyed the piece of comedy immensely at Ralph's expense and were whooping it up with all their might. It had been great fun for them but as I stood there I wondered why the other two lads had not come for breakfast.

I grabbed my mitts and hurried towards the point where Ralph had just disappeared in order to confirm that all was well with our three adventurers. As I rounded the corner I beheld a sight I will always carry with me till my parting breath. There on the snow some distance ahead lay a flat object that resembled the shape of a human form, rigid and covered in a layer of white frost. My heart skipped a beat as I drew closer and confirmed in my mind that this indeed was a human body frozen stiff on the surface of the lake. That meant but one thing, one of the boys had frozen to death on the ice through the night.

I covered the remaining distance in a trance and then stared down at a still, stiff form that lay at my feet. This was the oldest of the brothers and his entire body was covered with a white snowy frost. His eyes appeared to be frozen shut and his eyebrows were as white as the surrounding snow. His mouth was clamped shut in a gray thin line. My mind was in a blur as I turned and looked towards the tepee where I could see Ralph and Joey sitting on a tree limb. Ralph was tugging at a leather work boot trying to pull it over one of his now frozen bare feet. Neither he nor Joey seemed to be the least concerned about Lloyd who lay only a few feet away probably dead.

What had happened? How was this possible? A cold sinking feeling lay in the pit of my stomach. Kneeling down beside the prostrate form I placed my hand on his neck hoping to feel a pulse. A wave of emotion swept over me and then a ray of hope as first one eyelid opened and then the other. The frozen form of the seventeen year old was still alive. Relief washed over me as he moved a little and then sat up slowly. When I asked him if he was alright he seemed to be cognizant and mumbled in the affirmative. He stood up slowly and began to walk stiffly towards the fire where the rest of the group sat eating.

The white form I watched move across the lake resembled a mummy recently released from a cold tomb. I turned to Ralph who was now pulling on the other frozen boot as I had some questions for him. Why had he been running barefoot across the ice and why had Lloyd been lying on the ice evidently all night? Finally he was able to get the boot on over his cold red foot and then without looking at me he headed for the distant fire mumbling words that I could not understand.

It did not take the trio long to reach the blazing fire where they began the process of thawing out. To endure the pain of feet and hands unthawing is know pain seldom felt. Excruciating pain beyond comprehension that one must endure to truly appreciate. Once the process has begun there is no turning back, it must be carried to the finish. I watched the boys faces contorted in agony as the blood slowly crept back in their fingers and toes as the heat from the fire crept through their body. Unable to stand still they ran around, jumping up and down flapping their arms against their bodies trying to endure the intense pain.

Lloyd began to explain over a cup of coffee how during the night the smoke became so thick inside the tepee that he decided to leave with his sleeping bag and park outside under the stars. He soon found the ice so cold he placed the whole bag underneath him. I have often wondered how he lived through the night. Some call it a mystery but I call it a miracle. Only God could keep this thin young man from freezing to death on a cold winter night on a frozen lake with only the clothes he wore and no warm pad under him.

As for Ralph that young, wild and reckless youth told me with his crooked little smile how his leather work boots had become soaked the day before from the snow and then froze stiff during the night. Thus when he attempted to put his feet in them in the morning it could not be done so with his feet freezing in the cold air he opted to run barefoot across the ice in hope of reaching the fire and warming them up while drying out his boots. However the pain became so great he could not bear it and decided to run back to the tepee. I took time to remind him that those who chose to challenge the rigors of the northern winter should dress warmly and never wear leather work boots.

Ralph had given it his best but proved to himself and all how vulnerable we are when not properly equipped. Our three young friends were exuberant and adventurous and willing to tackle the great outdoors under extreme conditions but to their detriment and our chagrin they indeed endured some of the most painful and life threatening experiences anyone could go through.

Thirty years have passed and I still have visions of those hair raising days of snow camping with the youth of which we were to go on more. And to let you know we did spend another day as the boys drilled more holes in different locations on the lake and always keeping the fire going and the never ending job of finding dead wood to burn. The following day was very cold and the fish were not inclined to take our bait and so after assembling more snow huts and standing around the fire the boys were looking forward to heading home to tell their parents some tall stories.

I believe Tim and I had fulfilled our mandate to bring them back home safe and wiser in the ways of the outdoors but only with God's grace and provision were we able to accomplish that. We had been kept safe from disaster by a power far greater than our own.

In closing I will mention one last thing. My wife made a comment the day after I arrived home. Something to the effect that my hair seemed to be turning gray prematurely and how could that be as I had so little stress in my life.

The End

Written by John Gearey
February 2012

The Bug

Visitors at Turkey Lake

"There it is luv!" I sang out in an excited voice as we pulled up on a small hill near Turkey Lake in our newly customized VW Beatle. Mary my hard working wife had spiced it up with bright blue paint on the doors and hood which blended well with the beige on the rest of the vehicle. The set of fifteen inch chunky truck tires on the back end set the buggy higher and gave it an added sense of worthiness.

On top of our little bush buggy we had attached two wooden racks on which perched our magnificent new monster canoe. (At least we felt it was big.) A full sixteen feet with a forty inch beam and built with the heaviest fiberglass known to man, and weighed close to a hundred pounds.

Now one might ask what would ever entice a man to purchase such a monstrosity especially when he planned to carry it through the bush. I will endeavor to explain if that is possible. Being in the mid 70's of the last century and I being a mere lad of thirty and not being fully of sound mind I believed I could carry any canoe over any hill that might ever come my way. I was as well equally convinced that we needed a safe strong canoe to paddle the lakes and fish the mighty waters situated in the Cambrian Shield where we lived.

Now here we were with our new prize looking down the path that led to the waters edge of Turkey Lake. Unhooking the canoe from the wooden rack we soon were able to heave it up on our shoulders and start down the beaten trail with the incredible weight forcing us forward. Please note the "we". For some unknown reason the canoe had grown far too heavy for a "mere" lad like I.

At the shoreline we dropped our burden and stood gasping for air and waited for our bodies to recover.

After a partial recovery we trudged back up the steep incline to our "buggy" and began to unload our gear. It took but a short time to set up our new three man tent and carefully place our sleeping bags and ground pads on the tent floor.

Finally the time had come for the real reason we had drove thirty dusty miles over a bumpy road filled with pot holes and huge rocks. Fishing! Yes and I could hardly wait to head out unto the lake and beat the water with a few of our newly bought lures. Quickly we grabbed the fishing rods, net, paddles and tackle and headed down the slope to our waiting canoe.

The anticipation of catching a few nice trout was always sweet especially when we arrived on the shores of a lake we had never fished. How many days had I spent dreaming of the moment when I would land the biggest brook trout ever caught on a fishing rod? So with each new lake there was always the possibility of that one mighty fish that would fulfill my life long desire.

With the enthusiasm and eagerness of youth we pushed off shore. We had great hope that this would be a wonderful week-end of fishing and canoeing.

And so as we paddled slowly out to deeper water all the cares of the world seemed to disappear like the mist over a lake as it gives way to the penetrating morning sun.

Everything seemed perfect in every way. We had made all the right twists and turns on the old logging road and the big green canoe had stayed attached to the roof racks. The roof racks had stayed attached to the bush buggy and the bush buggy had stayed attached to the big knobby wheels. The day was sunny with no rain in the forecast and not another human being in sight.

The truth being that it was quite important to me to be alone on the lake with no other humans in sight. I felt that to enjoy the wilderness, the serenity and the whole outdoor experience to the highest degree there should not be another person in a twenty mile radius of the area. As well I felt the lake we planned to fish should have been untouched for at least the past ten years. However we already knew that Turkey Lake was far from pristine and at any time we could have visitors roll in and totally destroy the wonderful ambiance of the day.

The sunlight shimmered on the clear sparkling water as I continued to paddle easily along. Mary in the bow of the canoe cast her small blue Cleo towards the shoreline. With a small plunking noise it entered the water a few inches below the overhanging cedar boughs that stretched out from the shore. I had my line extended far behind the canoe and was trailing a large silver spinner and a gob of worm. The trout had little chance of resisting these spectacular presentations as we moved quietly through the water. A lunker of gigantic proportions would soon strike one of the lures and we then would have a delicious meal of fried speckled trout. Mmmm.

A light wind arose on the lake but the paddling was easy and all was peaceful. What more could we ask for? The sun was shining with hardly any wind and we had the lake all to ourselves with a big fish somewhere below just waiting to be caught. What a day to be out in the great outdoors.

One hour slipped away. This was truly a lovely picturesque lake, but no bites. Two hours went by. The intriguing shoreline beckoned us to cast into the many lurking shadows under the overhanging trees, but still no fish. Another hour passed as mid day approached and we paddled along in the warm sun as it reflected off the surface of the water but not one strike. We made it around the lake finally. My eyes had now begun to hurt, my head throbbed and my arms ached however we had enjoyed the time as we trolled and cast and rubbed our rears raw on the hard plastic seats of the canoe. Four hours on the lake and no fish for supper. At least we had the whole weekend ahead of us to look forward to and all the fun of outdoor cooking, resting in a peaceful campsite and to-morrow catching a pile of fish or perhaps that big one.

We landed our vessel and were disembarking when we heard

a strange noise. We stopped to listen and stood very still. There it was again coming from somewhere close to where we had set up camp.

"Craaack, Crack." The sound was similar to two paddles being struck together.

Our hearts skipped a beat.

"What was that noise?" Mary asked, "Is someone setting up camp near us?"

"No," I responded, my heart was beating more rapidly and Mary could hear the faint sign of trepidation in my voice. "It sounds like a bear, not a human."

"No, it can't be!" she murmured

"I'm pretty sure, luv, remember the big male we saw on the way in. There's probably a lot of bear in this area."

We began to walk up the path hoping against hope it wasn't Mr. Bruin. As we came up over the last rise we could see the bush buggy and fifty feet away our new little tent. Unfortunately it was lying on the ground and appeared to have been torn up and looked a mess from where we stood. Some of the tent poles were broken and others torn out of the ground. However there was no sign of whatever had caused the destruction. With some fear we slowly walked into the campsite looking each way to be sure our visitor had left the area. The evidence seemed to indicate that indeed it had been a bear and now it came to mind that we had left a can of carnation milk open just inside the tent door when we left. That had not been a clever move. True to nature our friend Yogi had smelled it and paid us a visit.

We began to breathe a little easier as we saw no sign of an animal so Mary proceeded to the vehicle while I headed over to the tent to take a closer look at the damage. The bear had entered from the front, ripping open the nylon mesh in its quest for the sweet milk. As I lifted parts of the tent and began examining the sleeping bags I began to smell a strong pungent odor that must have come from the bear as it rubbed its rear end all over our brand new sleeping bags.

As I continued my inspection a sound came to me from the direction of the Beetle, not unlike that of a faint whisper. I was on my knees and looked over to where Mary was standing.

"Honey, Honey!" there was a strange urgency to the whisper. "There's a bear standing right behind you!"

I could feel the hair on the back of my neck stand straight out. For the first time I had a real concern for our safety, some call it 'scared out of your wits'. My next thought was whether I could make it to the vehicle before the bear pounced on me and started beating me up. How wonderful the thoughts of self preservation are at times like these. I stood up slowly and decided to take a step towards Mary and the buggy. I had no real desire to turn and look at the bear. One's mind can do funny things when fear is involved.

Suddenly the thought came to me that maybe, just maybe Mary was pulling a prank and there was no bear behind me. Would she do such a thing? No, not possible I thought.

Very slowly I took one step at a time away from the wrecked tent without looking back. As I came closer to my wife who was standing by the vehicle I could no longer stand the suspense and looked back over my shoulder. Not a bear in sight. Where was the bear? It must have slipped silently into the bush as I had not heard a noise. Or had it? That old doubt reared its head again. Maybe it was never there. I took a close look at my loving wife and wondered. No she was not the kind of person that would scare the wits out of me. Then again it would be a great prank.

"What should we do now?" she asked.

"We will have to pack up, even though I hate leaving. The tent is ripped apart and the bear stunk up our sleeping bags something horrible" I moaned.

"Okay, let's pick up the gear and put it back in the V.W." she replied with a tint of sadness.

Our week-end trip that had started so well was now lost as we began to plan to go home. All the planning we had done earlier and the preparation was for nothing. Even the long dusty ride in had been for naught. Well we had been given a beautiful day and had canoed for several hours so we could be thankful for that but now we were being forced to leave this fine place and what really hurt was that we had not caught a single fish. Now that may sound somewhat trivial in the light of how much worse things could be and so I needed to be thankful the bear had not attacked us and that there was lots of daylight left to pack up and leave.

We were fortunate that we had left the cooler and other food in the locked vehicle and the bear had not found it. Two things had to happen before we could go home. First we had to collect up the tent and the sleeping bags and pads and put them in the buggy and next we had to trot down the path to the lake and retrieve the canoe and paddles, then bring them up and strap the canoe on the wooden racks of the little bush buggy.

Scanning the bush about us we neither heard nor saw any sign of the bear. We hoped it had left. We listened carefully for any sound but the forest was very still. Slowly I made my way back to the mangled tent. With some urgency and trepidation I pulled out the sleeping bags and pads and hurried back. Mary then came with me to collect up the tent and poles and pegs while watching nervously the surrounding area. We still were concerned our friend was nearby.

As we finished jamming all the gear in the backseat we heard a noise a few feet away at the front right fender of the car. We both turned and found ourselves face to face with a mother bear and her cub. Only a short fifteen feet away they were standing together simply staring at us, probably wondering why we were leaving and if we had anymore of that delicious sweet milk. They looked so cute and inquisitive and I wondered how long they had been there.

Mary and I had been loading the gear from the passenger side of the Beetle when we noticed our friends.

At the sight of Mrs. Bear and offspring Mary jumped into the passenger seat and closed the door without saying a word. That left me, old Johnny boy standing out in the cold so to speak, with nothing to do but converse with Mama and child and I was not sure what frame of mind they were in.

I grabbed the door and said with a controlled voice, "Quick move over."

I did not want to attempt to run around the car and get in the drivers side as it might upset the animals.

"No," came the reply from inside.

I couldn't believe it. "What do you mean, no!" I responded in disbelief. Was this the woman who said she loved me and would lay down her life for me. Now I was frantic.

"Move over quick." I squeaked again

"No, I can't move over," she said once more. "The consul shifter is in the way."

"So what!" I cried, "Climb over it and hurry!"

She still wouldn't move.

Having no other choice I began to move very slowly towards the back of the vehicle while keeping an eye on the bears. I was ready for a dash to the car door when a question came to mind. Did I unlock that side of the car? If not, Mama Bear would have me dancing to her wishes if she chose to have some fun.

Making it around the end of the bush buggy I looked back at the bears. They were gone! Again they had slipped silently away into the nearby bush. The close encounter had ended well with our friendly bears, however I wondered where they would appear next.

The final task was to go back down to the water and retrieve the monster canoe and secure it to the racks. I carefully scrutinized the dense bush about us. The thick green foliage of spring offered many places to hide our furry visitors.

"Let's get at it," I mumbled as I prepared myself for the job ahead. I looked at Mary through the side glass window to see if maybe she might give me a helping hand. She had no intention of moving from her secure position inside the closed doors of the Beetle. I would have to bring that great hulk of a canoe up that steep trail by myself. What was I thinking when I bought that monstrosity!

With a nervous step and a faint heart I headed down the hill.

Still no sign of the bears but I wondered if they were watching and preparing to step out in front of me in hopes of getting a hand out. I arrived at the shoreline and hoisted the canoe up on my shoulders and started back up. For the next few moments the bears were forgotten as I staggered forward under the weight of my prize possession. I stumbled the last few feet to the waiting vehicle with my lungs wheezing and shoulders aching and managed to slide the canoe unto the racks. Gasping for air I looked around and then began to tie it down.

At this point Mary decided to open her door and step out most likely thinking she would give me a hand to tie down the straps.

There were no bears in sight at the moment. I secretly hoped she felt guilty. As we went about tightening the straps and tying down the ropes she happened to look up and there once more standing on the road staring at us were our two friendly bears. And sure enough Mary disappeared inside the Beatle once again.

Hastily I finished the knot I was tying and jumped in behind the wheel.

"Friendly little cuss's," I chirped as I looked over at them.

"Let's get out of here," Mary replied.

"Yeah, good idea luv, sure hope this thing goes." I muttered hoping to put some anxiety in her heart. I still remembered her leaving me out with the bears.

She glanced over at me with a look of dismay. I chuckled to myself as I knew my comment had worked.

Pushing down on the clutch I pulled the choke and turned the key.

"Brrrrrr------brrrrrrr," the engine tried to turn over. I looked over at my dear wife with a doubtful expression. Now she was really concerned. I was grinning inside. I turned the key one more time.

"Brrrrrr------Frrrrr-------Froom!" The old V.W. started. The look of relief washed over her face as she listened to the purring of the motor and I silently gave thanks.

A moment later we were bounding down the road in our little Bug and one huge canoe perched on top, waving good-bye to our furry black friends.

The end

Written by John Gearey
Aug. 2002

Rick and Chico

Trouble at Surf Lake

Autumn lay on the hills of Superior. The maple trees had developed a tinge of orange with a scattering of red patches. The leaves of the white birches were still partially green but had begun to pale to a faded yellow. It was a time for reflection and solitude, a time of peace and resignation as the forest prepared to change its summer coat for its fall ensemble.

Four men stood at the base of a steep hill on a portage that led to Surf Lake preparing themselves mentally for the hard climb ahead.

"There it is fellows, Heartattack Hill or so I call it. Last time I went up here with the canoe and pack I thought I was going to die." sang out John, a man who had been over this trail several times in the past few years. Now in his forties he still enjoyed these trips and the challenges that came with them but knew they were getting tougher for him each year.

The four men had dropped their packs and canoes and moved up for a closer look at the first grade. Eli was standing close to him and was a friend who was now in his mid fifties had never been on this trail before but seemed unaffected by what he viewed ahead. He looked back at the two younger men that stood behind them. Rick and Chico were long time friends in their early thirties and together with John had been on several trips into the interior of Lakes Superior Park south of the town of Wawa. Both men loved fishing and camping and the hill ahead was but a small obstacle they would easily overcome in order to get to their destination.

Eli looked over at John and smiled. "We'll make it."

The morning was now half gone and the group had already

traversed two lakes, one stream and a long portage to get to this point. John took a long drink from an old canteen he had slung around his neck and walked back to the others. Rick stood beside an old partially painted canoe that bore signs of better days. Bits of green paint were flaking off the sides while the underside was white with bare spots. Chewing slowly on a granola bar he looked up as his friend approached. His coal black hair crept out below the ball cap that partially covered the well tanned face of a man who enjoyed the sun.

Rick nodded at John and then motioned towards Eli.

"Will Eli be alright going up that hill?"

They were all aware that their friend had recently come through major neck surgery.

"Aw, he'll be fine" replied John softly. He knew his partner was strong and in good condition. Eli came towards them slowly peeling an orange. Separating it into sections he offered each one a piece, then turned and picked up his pack. John swallowed his orange and without a word hoisted his pack on his back. Clutching the canoe by the gunwales he flipped it up on his shoulders and without hesitation headed for the first rise. Eli followed a short distance behind. He walked slowly and methodically, pausing at times to catch his breath. A short two years past he had undergone open heart surgery to repair an aneurysm in his aorta valve and then a year later neck surgery. He hoped his heart was up to this kind of workout.

He watched John ahead of him staggering along and began laughing to himself. He wondered how he was able to keep going with those two banty legs, and carry the low slung packsack on his back with the canoe swaying from side to side.

Far below came the muffled sounds of Rick and Chico as they began their ascent up the tortuous hill. Their old canoe was much heavier than John's and they were reaching deep within to find the strength to climb this steep hill while gasping for air and muttering under their breath about a friend that would ask them to climb something like this.

After some time and a lot of sweat the four made it to the top and took a rest. Shortly they moved on down the portage to Connell Lake. Once on the lake they took their time and paddled leisurely watching for sign of rising trout.

"Smack," a loud noise from behind the canoe jolted John from his quiet contemplation. For a brief moment he was a young boy on the farm again and the kitchen door had just slammed shut behind him. Turning to look with increased heartbeat he caught sight of a large flat tail disappearing beneath the surface of the water.

"What was that?" asked Eli, twisting in his seat to look back.

"Beaver, a big one. Guess he's telling us to get out of his territory." John replied with a sheepish grin. The noise had startled him more than he wished to admit.

The paddle across Connell lake was short and the portage between Connell and Surf Lake was shorter still. All four travelers felt relaxed as they paddled down Surf Lake towards the far end where they would set up camp.

As the afternoon grew to a close, the men had hoisted two tents high on a promontory above the water.

Off to one side of the clearing a tarp covered a stack of dry cedar kindling and a quantity of dry birch bark. Close by several round logs had been carefully piled in readiness for the evening fire. A circular fire pit had been dug with a large number of rocks set around it. The men now fatigued from the days exertion sat on the decaying stumps around the pit chewing on a few snacks that had been hidden in their pockets.

Chico who had been staring at the lake for some time suddenly got up and assembled his fishing rod, and grabbed his fishing lures he headed down a steep path to a rock ledge below where he made a cast far out into the water. He was a man who enjoyed the wilderness and the thrill of a trout on the end of line. Strong, resilient with great stamina he was a valuable companion to have on any trip.

"Let's try some fishing from the canoe." Rick suggested as he came down the path towards Chico.

"Good idea," Chico replied as he reeled in his line. "It's going to be a little rough out there."

The wind had increased and was hurling large waves up against the rocky ledge they stood on.

The pair were soon in the canoe and heading into the wind. Eli and John watched them for some time as they paddled furiously against the wind and waves.

"Maybe we should try that bay on the west side, Eli before dark. The wind won't be nearly as strong in there." John commented.

Eli looked at the threatening sky and the approaching darkness. "Sure." he muttered, not quite sure he wanted to fight the wind and waves.

A few minutes later the bow of the canoe was cutting through the water spraying over the bow. John let out a few feet of line behind the canoe with a lure and worm attached. Placing the rod and reel between his feet he continued to paddle steadily while letting out line. Eli made a cast against the wind and then grabbed a paddle to help keep the canoe angled into the waves. They had come into a protected cove not far from the camp when Eli felt a hard tug on his rod. John held the canoe steady as his friend brought a struggling brook trout up alongside the canoe and netted it.

Rick and Chico appeared around a far point not far distant paddling with measured strokes. They worked hard at angling the canoe in the waves and kept their paddles in the water much of the time for better balancing. This was not a time to have a flip over. An hour had passed and they had managed to land two small trout. Within minutes they steered into the small bay and towards their partners.

"We're heading in." yelled Chico.

"Yeah we are too, its far too rough out here and I'm tired." John called back.

Sometime later flames from the firepit leaped around the bottom of two large cans filled with water that hung from a suspended pole. Hermetically sealed aluminum pouches held the men's supper which they fondly called "Magic Pantry's" the name of the makers. To-night the menu would be cabbage rolls, steak and vegetables and lasagna. All to be washed down with strong black tea. The pouches were immersed in the boiling water for five minutes and the food was ready to eat.

"Man, am I hungry," John said as he watched the water boil. He was not only hungry but incredibly tired as well. He took an extra pouch of food out of his sack and slipped it into the water. He was ravenous and one more steak would really hit the spot.

The night closed around them as the four sat eating their supper and watched the flames throw licks of yellow and orange tongues into the air, while the wind sent puffs of smoke skyward.

They talked while they ate and periodically waved their hands at the curling smoke that enveloped them, rubbing their eyes or turning away from the fire. After supper it was not long before the comfort of their sleeping bags beckoned them. Rick was the first to stand and announce his departure and head for his tent. Chico followed shortly after.

The wind had begun to subside as John and Eli sat listening to the sounds of the night time, each lost in his thoughts. John felt stuffed after the large meal. He decided to walk around and do some light calisthenics to relieve the heavy feeling in his stomach. Eli climbed into the tent and began rustling around preparing to go to sleep. His partner stood outside for some time. John felt a deep weariness come over him, a tiredness like he seldom had felt before. He knew he had to lie down to get the rest he needed, but he felt uncomfortably full and wondered if he would be able to fall asleep. The night air was beginning to chill him. With one last look at the red hot coals in the firepit he slipped through the mesh door of the tent.

Discarding his clothes at the foot of the small tent he climbed into his sleeping bag.

"How do you feel Eli?" John asked as he closed his eyes and laid his head on his jacket.

"Okay. Why?" came a muffled tired voice from the sleeping bag next to him.

"Just wondered, I'm feeling really stuffed."

John laid back down and listened to the soft lapping of the waves on the rocks below and slipped quietly into sleep.

"Ra-ta-ta-la-la-booty-boom boom."

He sat straight upright in his bag, his eyes still shut, but his heart pounding.

"What's that racket?" he yelled looking towards where Eli was laying.

"It's my radio." came the voice inside the sleeping bag next to him.

"Your radio? Your radio? Why would ever bring a radio all the way in here?" John asked harshly.

"What's wrong with that?" Eli responded not moving.

John laid back and grunted. "I never bring a radio, I like to leave civilization behind me."

"Well I like to listen to the news and weather." chomped his friend.

"That's fine for you, but that noise woke me and I need to sleep." John grumbled and rolled over.

A sigh of disgust came from within Eli's sleeping bag, then silence. Both men slept.

Time passed peacefully for the four tired men in their comfortable settings. They were oblivious to the muffled hoot of an owl from across the bay and the lonesome cry of a loon from far down the lake.

Suddenly John sat bolt upright for the second time that night. Something was wrong. His groggy mind tried to function. He felt ill, very ill. He knew he had to get out of the tent and fast. Fumbling with the zipper on his sleeping bag he managed to roll out and crawl to the door. Grasping his small flashlight he frantically worked to open the tent door zipper. He shoved his feet into his boots and without tying them up he scrambled outside.

The man now stood with only his shorts on in the cold night

air. His whole body felt sick. Shining the light ahead of him he headed for the edge of the clearing and then made his way into the bush beyond.

Stopping he leaned forward and began to throw up violently. He had never been this sick on a wilderness trip before. He tried to focus and control himself, but was overwhelmed by dizziness. Again and again he threw up. Trying to maintain his balance on the hill he found himself surrounded by trees when he began to have attacks of diarrhea. Misery filled his body. What was wrong? Was this to be the end of his tenure on earth, here on the side of a hill deep in Superior Park all alone in the dark?

Weakness was overcoming him. His legs were rubbery and his strength almost gone as he squatted perilously with his pants around his ankles among the thorny bushes waiting for the next attack. Suddenly without warning one foot slipped sideways and he rolled down into a small depression. Branches ripped at his bare flesh as he tried to right himself. Beginning to shake from exposure and the illness he knew he had to find his way back to the campsite. It felt as if he'd been out here for an hour.

The upheavals were subsiding but he felt cold all over and still felt ill. He began to slowly grope his way back to the clearing. He could barely see the glow from the embers of the fire through the bush that surrounded him. Dropping to his knees in front of the tent he peaked inside.

Eli was sleeping and that was a good thing. He felt he might be sick again at any time but was dead tired and knew he must get warm and get some sleep.

Slowly he crawled into the tent and slid into his bag. Laying his head down he felt a wave of dizziness come over him. Quickly he sat up and propped himself against the back of the tent. He might start throwing up again lying prostrate so he tried sitting upright and closing his eyes.

"Agh." Opening his eyes quickly. No good he thought trying to overcome the sick feeling and relax. He sat still hoping sleep would come and his body would come back to normal.

Hearing a small snort next to him, John turned and looked over at the man sleeping next to him.

"Great," he moaned. "I'm dying and he's resting like a baby."

An hour passed while he sat with his head bowed on his chest fighting off waves of dizziness. Finally total fatigue overcame him and he slumped over in an exhausted enhanced sleep.

Morning arrived with large dark clouds threatening overhead and the wind had begun to howl as the day before. Both tent flys had ballooned far out and seemed ready to tear the anchor pegs out of the ground. The tents shook with each great gust. Chico was the first to emerge and promptly began to round up some small branches and birch bark for a fire. Stirring the still warm coals he was able to get a small flame started under the pile of sticks. He loved the fires and loved setting them up and his buddies always appreciated his willingness to get things going. Rick emerged from his tent.

"Keep it going Cheek." he called out and began to hang two cans of water above the small fire.

"Tough day to fish boys." Eli muttered as he climbed out of his tent, looking well rested.

"Where's that Johnny boy?" sang out Chico.

"I'm coming," John murmured appearing behind Eli. "You all didn't here me last night?"

Each one shook their heads. "I thought I was a goner, for sure." he said quietly and slumped down on the nearest stump.

"You're as pale as a ghost John." Chico remarked looking his friend over.

"I still don't feel well, but I'll live. It must have been the food or maybe the exhaustion. Who knows."

John stared at the fire before him. He still felt unwell.

Once the water was boiled the men drank instant coffee and

chewed on breakfast bars and fruit. The hot drink warmed the sick man as he felt it work its way down but he felt weak and dizzy.

"Are you well enough to go out fishing to-day?" Eli asked studying his partner.

"Give me a little while to recover and I should be okay." came the response.

John sat very still staring into the mug of hot liquid he held between his shaking hands.

The wind continued to buffet the group as they huddled around the little fire.

"Do you want to try some fishing, Chico?" Rick asked looking out at the wind swept lake.

"Sure, but it'll be plenty rough." came the reply.

The pair headed down to the waiting canoe that had been pulled far up on the rocks. Without hesitation they slipped the craft into the water and headed into the waves.

Eli and John stood high above the water and watched their friends paddle briskly into the white caps. The wind was harsh and cold and drove the two men back to the comfort of the small fire. John still felt weak and the cup of coffee and piece of toast had not made him feel any better. Eli seemed restless and moved about the campsite cleaning up.

"Are you up for a short paddle?" he asked "Maybe we'll catch a couple of those big ones you've been telling me about."

Something between a chuckle and a grunt was forthcoming.

With a little effort John forced himself to walk to the canoe on the ledge below which held their fishing gear. He wondered if he had the strength to give this a real try. The wind was high and came straight at them as they pushed off. Paddling hard they headed for the safety of the bay they had been in the previous night. Eli put his paddle down and made several casts toward the nearest shore. Moving down the bay they continued to cast and troll for the next hour. The wind harried them relentlessly, the waves bashing against the side of the small canoe. Nearing a rocky point they could see the other craft with Rick and Chico being swept along. Chico had caught sight of them and was pointing towards the campsite on the hill. They were heading in.

"Ready to go in Eli?" John yelled.

"Sure, I've had enough of this wind for now." came the reply.

John swung the canoe up against the swells and hurled past the jut of land to the right of them.

Eli put his fishing rod down and was paddling with deep strong strokes. For a brief instant they seemed to hang in mid air from a large swell and then they were dropped into a pocket of water ahead with the bow buried in the wave. John frantically attempted to carve the canoe in the direction of camp as the next swell lifted them high. They survived the turn up against the wind and now were being thrust forward in the right direction with the wind in their backs. The sun was still high in the sky as the fishermen sailed their craft far up on the rocky beach below their tents.

Their two friends had landed moments earlier and were busy carrying their gear up the trail.

"Any fish guys?" John asked.

"Only a couple. It is far too rough down the lake." Chico responded. "How about you guys?"

"We got two small ones in the bay." Eli answered as he flipped the canoe over on the rocks.

"I'll try to get this fire going so we can have some tea. I feel chilled." Rick yelled from further up the trail.

"I'll clean the fish." Chico was coming down with his fillet knife in his hand. "Throw me those minnows guys." he yelled.

Not long after the four men were huddled once more in a circle around the fire hoping to catch some warmth. The small meal was over and they sat holding their steaming mugs of hot drink and discussed better days and great fishing tales as fishermen are wont to do when sitting around a fire with a drink in hand.

John looked over at the tent. The morning outing had drained what little energy he had and now he felt exhausted to the point of collapse. He knew he should get in his sleeping bag and have a rest. Chico sat opposite him, munching slowly on a dried piece of jerky and watched his friend. He finished his drink and stood up.

"I'm going to lie down for a while John and by the looks of you, you should too." he rasped and headed for his tent.

John looked up at the white billowy clouds moving rapidly across the blue sky. Eli had taken the cue and made his way to his tent. The time had come to recuperate.

"It looks like we're all headed for a rest big guy." John commented as he looked over at Rick still seated by the fire.

"Go ahead my man, I'm going to sit and relax here for awhile and enjoy this drink."

Richard watched his friends disappear one by one into the confines of their tents. He could feel the harsh wind on his stubbled face as he gazed across the nearest bay. The maple trees on the nearest hill were swaying from the gusts that came in sporadic bursts.

He sensed a strong call to explore the surrounding area and locate a path he knew led to another lake some two miles away. The sound of rushing wind through the trees called to him and with a lurch forward he headed for the nearby tree line. He soon found himself following a faint animal trail that led around the nearest bay. Being curious as to where the trail might lead to he continued on. He watched for signs of beaver or other kinds of wild life when he spotted a small stream a short distance to his right. The water quietly rippled over the stones and in a shallow pool he could see several small trout darting for cover as he approached.

In the tree tops the wind blew with great bursts of power shaking the large maples on the hill side and bending the tall spruce trees that grew closer to the lake.

Rick's curiosity drove him on and all thoughts of the wind and time were swept away as he followed the old trail. He hoped he would find the logging road he had been on a year ago that led to the next lake. As he began to move further from the bay he was struck by the changing autumn scene that surrounded him, the smell of fallen rotting leaves and old wood. A large ruffed grouse suddenly burst into a clearing directly in front of him and his heart jumped. He regretted not having his 22 rifle, they might have a taste of meat along with the trout for supper.

Onward he went but was finding the path increasingly hard to follow. Peering far ahead he thought he could make out a small clearing. Leaving the dim trail he headed towards a sparsely treed opening barely visible where the sunlight was penetrating. Looking back he could no longer see water but felt he could still find his way back to camp without too much trouble.

With no compass or map Rick tried to assure himself he would not get disoriented as long as he returned the way he came. Crossing the small opening he moved on hoping to find some of the old ribbons and slash marks they had made last year that would help him find the logging road. He felt it would only be a short distance and should be able to locate it quickly. In his mind he was sure he was going in the right direction.

Twenty minutes later unable to find any sign of the road he was looking for he decided to head back to camp. Looking skyward he could see the sun peeking through the clouds and noted it was much lower and further to the west.

Something was gnawing away at his thoughts. He no longer was sure in what direction to head. Noting the time, he felt he could make it back to camp before supper. Quickening his pace he moved down into a small depression and walked across a soggy grass filled bog that caused him to sink over his running shoes.

Moving to higher ground that held a variety of hardwoods he cast his eyes about not sure in what direction to go. A premonition of impending doom had begun to come over him. He had lost his bearings and was lost. A sinking feeling in the pit of his stomach propelled him forward with far greater haste.

Then without any advance notice he stumbled unto an old overgrown logging road.

Could this be the same road they had been on the previous year? No, it couldn't be. This road was too overgrown with no sign of traffic except for moose prints. Well it was wide enough and had been used for truck traffic in years past. Maybe it was the same road but he didn't know which way to head. One way led to a lake two miles away and the other way was five or six miles to the highway. Either one would mean at least one night in the bush and what if this road was a different road and lead nowhere.

Confusion was mounting in his mind as he tried to decide what to do. He knew he could be out here for days with no food or good water wandering about in the daytime and sleeping on the cold ground at night with near zero temperatures. And what if it rained he would most likely succumb to hypothermia and exposure.

An idea came to him. If someone was looking for him from the air they might not see him but they might see markings. Grabbing a stick he began carving out a huge S.O.S. sign on an open patch of sand near the center of the logging road.

A touch of trepidation had invaded his being as he made a decision to leave the road and try to find his way back the way he had come. With his eyes on the ground he searched for the small trail he had followed. Time was passing and he had become increasingly more frantic and often tripped over dead tree limbs and branches that had fallen during past wind storms.

Pausing for a moment to catch his breath he thought of the many years of traipsing through the bush and never being lost. And now here he was, alone and lost in the centre of this great expanse of wilderness, with no compass on an overcast day and only a cold and windy night to look forward to. A sudden wave of panic hit him as he realized the dilemma he was in and what the outcome could easily be. What if he was headed the wrong direction and missed the lake?

Rushing forward with his heart pounding and his breath coming in great gasps all he could see around him were trees, trees and more trees. Hill after hill of trees and above the trees he could hear the wind howling and moaning. His mind was racing. How could this happen? How could he be so foolish to take off without a compass? He wished he could see the sun but it was covered by dark gray clouds. Fear gripped his chest like a giant vice. He knew he must stop this panic attack and the headlong rush through the woods.

Should he fall and break a leg he would never make it out and no one would ever find him.

Seeing a log he knelt down and catching his breath he began to pray. He had always believed in God but now his faith was being tested as never before. Visions of dying of starvation and exposure filled his mind as he cried out to God for help. He prayed more fervently than ever before that God would lead him back to the lake.

Thoughts of his wife and boy, his father, mother and siblings and friends came to him as he knelt there. How he wished he could tell them how much he cared for them at this moment. Now he knew how vulnerable each one is when in the grasp of nature and away from the protection of community. He wondered if his friends back at camp had begun to worry about him. Perhaps they had realized he was lost and had spread out in the bush looking for him. However they as well would be in jeopardy of getting lost.

He was in big trouble but knew he must keep moving. Hauling himself up he turned and looked over his shoulder. Staring through the endless trees he thought he saw something blue. Could that be water? A pang of hope surged through him. If that was water it might be another lake and not Surf Lake.

Striding down a steep hill he kept his eyes on the blue color that was becoming larger. He looked carefully for any sign or tree that might be familiar and continued praying that the water ahead was indeed the lake the campsite was on. Ahead of him in a small valley he could make out a small stream. As he drew closer he was sure it was the same brook he had crossed earlier in the day. Could it be? Hope renewed his spirit. If indeed this was the way he had come God had answered his cry for help and was showing him the way back. He lost sight of what had appeared to be water but he still felt sure he was headed in the right direction.

Following the stream he soon came upon a worn path heading towards the blue he had seen through the trees. Rick looked heavenward and thanked God, then pushed his way forward through the brush and tag alders. As he broke out of the heavy brush he could see a clearing on a knoll and the dark outlines of human figures. A strong whiff of burning wood came to his nostrils.

He rushed forward into the campsite with a great sigh of relief.

Emotions of joy overcame him as his three companions came running to meet him. The expressions of anxiety were quickly replaced by the look of relief on their faces.

They had come to the conclusion he was lost and had been in a quandary of what to do the last few hours.

When they awoke he was gone and when he didn't come back they tried to decide on what to do to find him. Without knowing the direction Rick had taken and with night approaching they simply stayed where they were hoping and praying he could find his own way out.

Rick settled on a stump and tried to explain why he had gone for a walk in the bush without a compass or map.

The remainder of the trip for the four men was one of fishing, resting and packing for the trip home. As we close this true story we must tell you that Rick was never the same man in the woods ever again. From that day till now he has been very cautious when hiking and always carries a map and compass and always gives God the thanks for his miraculous guidance back to his friends.

The End

Written by John Gearey
April 2012

John and Mary

A Life and Death Grip

The young man was barely twenty-one years old and his wife only nineteen when they made a trip to the northern region of the province of New Brunswick in the mid sixties to visit relatives and do a little fishing in the rivers and streams. Little did they realize what was about to happen while fishing one of the larger streams.

This story comes in two parts, one on a small river and the other on a steep cliff in Ontario and the tale could easily be called "Returning a Favour." Life and death are often but moments apart. While enjoying the outdoors this young couple found early on that potential disaster awaits when caution is not taken.

Part One

The day was sunny with a small breeze furling the leaves on the maple trees as the man and woman carried their small canoe and fishing equipment across a large field and through the brush to a wide and surging stream. John was tall and thin and stayed in good condition by running long distance for a past time. His wife Mary as well was strong and light in weight. She had gone on several fishing trips with her hubby and they both enjoyed the outdoors and catching fish.

Placing their canoe on the shore of the swift running stream the couple put on their life jackets and John put on a pair of hip waders. He planned to stop along the way and wade downstream and fish the pockets of deep holes that would be too difficult to do from the canoe due to the speed of the current.

Once they were ready they climbed into their craft and caught the first set of small rapids that emptied into a large pool that looked as if it would have trout. Casting about with worms and small spinners they landed two nice fish and then they were off to the next bend of the river.

The large stream was beautiful with many crooks and turns and small rapids with a number of small beaches. These beaches were usually either pebble or sand where fishermen would often land for a respite and enjoy sitting in the sand or walk about casting in the swirls of a pool close by in the hope of landing the big one.

As the day progressed the man and wife caught several good sized trout and John stashed them in a small creel he had brought for that purpose. Many of the streams and rivers in this area held brook trout of all sizes and in great abundance during the sixties and early seventies of the twentieth century due to the light fishing pressure.

The small canoe they were in had a narrow beam and a rounded bottom so they had to be careful when in the swift parts of the stream especially the time being mid May and the water barely above freezing.

Sometime in the mid afternoon the couple knew they were getting close to the lake the small river emptied into. John steered the craft unto a small beach and climbed out in order to try a few casts under an overhang not far ahead. A large trout burst from beneath a hidden log and the fight was on. The fish zigzagged from one side of the pool to the other but the thrashing trout was soon brought to net.

"Let's head down the next set of rapids and we should see the lake once we go around the next bend." John said to his wife as he pushed off shore and jumped in. The hip waders had seen lots of use this day, cumbersome at times but had kept his legs and feet dry. He was sure glad he had brought them. Hopefully there were one or two more spots he could try before they came to the lake.

The stream picked up speed and narrowed as they came into a sharp bend. The bow of the canoe suddenly hesitated as if something had grabbed it from below.

As the back end swept sideways Mary yelled, 'Watch out hon, we're going over!" and in the twinkling of an eye the two were sent into the frigid spring waters of the northern waterway. She hung on to the bow the best she could as they were hurled down the rapids sideways close to shore. Looking back she saw her husband hanging desperately on to the stern.

As the shoreline swept by Mary tried to grab the bushes and tag alders growing out over the edges of the stream. The ice cold water had begun to penetrate her outer garments and she could feel her body temperature dropping and knew she must find a place to get out and quickly. She looked back at John who didn't seem to be making any effort to swim or help her move the craft to shore.

"Are you okay?" she managed to spit out.

"Not really" came a mumbled reply, "I can't move my legs and I'm sinking slowly. If I let go of the canoe I will drown as I'm unable to tread water with these hip waders on."

Her mind was racing as she looked back at the swiftly moving shoreline and then she saw a small opening under an overhanging bush. With two strong side strokes she came close enough to grasp a large branch. Letting her feet down she found bottom and while still hanging onto the bow of the canoe she threw herself forward up unto the embankment.

Behind her the stern of the canoe moved downstream with John clinging to the slippery gunwale. The weight of the water that had filled his hip waders was pulling him lower and he was losing strength. He had unsnapped the waders from his belt but couldn't pull them down. Mary continued to pull herself up on the small soggy bank of the stream while keeping a hand the canoe.

"Come on hon, try moving up along the side of the canoe while I hold unto it." she said calmly as she gripped the bow with all her might.

"I don't know if I can," he replied, his eyes had taken on a frantic look. "I'm losing strength and can't move."

"Stay calm luv you can do it, just get close enough and I'll get a hold of you." Mary tried to pull harder on the canoe but it would not move.

Using all his willpower John began inching his way closer to shore. He knew time was running out as the water filled waders kept pulling him down and then he felt something solid under his feet and pushed another foot forward trying to reach Mary's outreached hand.

"A little further and I'll be able to grab you." she said.

"Keep hold of that canoe luv or you'll be walking back through the bush soaking wet and could succumb to hypothermia. He knew she could not hold the canoe much longer.

Mary swung her arm out further and felt John's hand come into hers. She gripped his hand with all she had and pulled using her weight trying to get him up to where he could manage himself.

John finally with a burst of strength fell forward half on the bank. He dragged himself up a foot at a time till he was out of the water and then the two pulled the canoe partly up on shore. A moment later he gave her a kiss and thanked her for saving his skin.

"What a grip you have hon," he mumbled as he began to pull off his waders. He had begun to shake a little now that he was out of the water. "A few more minutes in there and I was a goner."

"It must have been the adrenalin babe," she replied as she pulled one of his boots off and the water spilled out. In a few minutes they had pulled the canoe up unto dry land and emptied it.

"We have to finish the river and get across the lake fast or we'll perish from the cold." he spouted, "It looks like we lost a paddle and all our gear, including the creel of fish."

"I see the other paddle lodged down by the next bend." Mary said. "Too bad about the fish but we're still alive."

"Let's be careful getting back in the canoe, it's treacherous right here to get back on the river but we have little choice." He said as he maneuvered the bow out into the fast current. "Jump in luv and we'll try again. Once we're on the lake we'll be in the sun and hopefully warm up enough so we can get down the lake."

With some trepidation they launched their shallow craft out into the swirling water and were sent quickly downstream. Mary reached out and grabbed the lodged paddle on the way by and they were off.

Thankfully the sun was still warm enough to help dry their clothes and they arrived safely on the shore of the small lake and then hiked back up the old logging road to pick up their vehicle.

What lessons can be learned from this near death experience for this young man and his wife? We all think we are invulnerable when young and full of excitement. Take time to consider all the safety issues involved when being in the outdoors.

For John he risked his life and maybe his wife's by wearing those hip waders while in a tipsy craft on a fast running stream. But for the grace of God and the grip of steel that Mary had this story could have ended differently.

More could be said but we will wait till the end of another adventure these two had in Part 2 of this story.

PART TWO

The small black Austin Healy Sprite pulled off the main road and down a dirt side road sliding in the loose gravel. A opening appeared ahead containing three picnic benches with a few trees and a giant cliff at one end of the area. Inside the tiny car John and Mary sat staring up at the hill before them which had a high steep rock face hundreds of feet high.

"Well hon we came to have a picnic and this is a great place, so I'll get out the basket of food and we can put the table cloth on one of those tables." chirped Mary.

John continued to stare up at the face of the cliff and seemed to be contemplating something. His wife now out of the car had grabbed the picnic basket and started towards a table yelling back to him.

"Come on and give me a hand and bring those soft drinks in the trunk."

Slowly he exited and taking the bottles from the back he scurried to catch up. The day was warm with a bright sun and slight breeze. The couple had been married only a short time and had recently come back from a trip to New Brunswick where they had visited relatives and enjoyed some excellent fishing. The memories of a near disaster on a small river had faded long ago and they looked forward to the excitement each day might bring.

After setting the table and preparing the food for lunch the pair sat on the wooden bench seats enjoying the day and the warmth of the sun. John commented almost to himself, "What do you say we do a little climbing after we eat luv? That cliff looks like it has a lot of hand holds and what a view we would have when we get to the top. What say? I'll go ahead and go up a ways first to make sure it's safe for you."

Mary always a little cautious turned and stared at the looming sheer wall of gray.

"I'm not sure I want to try that, but it would be a great view alright. You go ahead and start when we're done eating and maybe I'll give it a try if it's not to difficult."

John wore a pair of half shorts and his wife a pair of cut-offs. Both wore running shoes with no socks and light t-shirts as the day was warm being the middle of August. He definitely knew this was not the right clothing to be wearing when free climbing a rock face but here they were and so typical to his make-up they would make the attempt with no ropes or other paraphernalia.

Neither of them considered safety harness's, pulleys, pitons, hooks or any other gear that could make their climb far safer.

Forty years ago technology was slowly developing some of these much needed devices but for John the challenge of climbing a sheer cliff with no safeties was exhilarating and so he eagerly strode to the base of the granite wall. He had strong hands and good balance and a load of confidence as he reached for the first small crevice above him. Pulling himself up to the next small ledge his right foot found leverage and he now was nearly ten feet off the ground. Looking down he could see Mary had finished putting the picnic basket away and was heading towards him looking up.

"There are a lot hand holds and foot holds hon and its not as steep as it looks." he said.

She looked up at him dubiously and surveyed the entire cliff. There definitely looked like several ledges to use. Well maybe she could do it she thought.

John watched her begin her climb and then he climbed higher while turning sideways at times to see how she was managing the first few feet. The parking area was deserted so they had no one watching them or making any comments as they climbed which he was pleased about. Steadily moving upwards he kept an eye on his young wife who was not accustomed to this type of outdoor activity and as a teenager had been involved only in skating and swimming. Still he was sure she could handle the climb with those strong and good looking legs that were one of the many attractions for him when he met her less than two years earlier.

Mary had moved sideways on the cliff finding her own path and not staying behind her husband but close enough they could communicate. Together they climbed higher and higher and then they reached a seeming impasse that stalled both of them as they now were only a few yards apart.

"I have to go around those rocks as I can't climb over them." John said as he viewed the jagged black rocks directly above him. You should come this way luv and be careful and follow me around the far side of this overhang."

Mary had two good foot holds and could see some small crevices for her to hang unto. John was already moving left to circumvent the trouble spot and seemed to be climbing quickly now. Looking below she could tell they had already climbed half way up the cliff but looking down was not a good thing as it made her feel a shade woosy. Using good hand holds and placing her feet carefully in shallow holes she was able to move sideways and upwards. She began to feel as if she was losing energy probably from the hot sun on her back.

The continuous tension on her legs had begun to take a toll and her fingers were tiring as well.

Looking upwards she could see the top of the cliff high above and would be glad to finish the climb.

Meanwhile John had moved up the side of the cliff and above his partner while keeping an eye on her progress. He could see she had come to a spot and had stopped climbing. The problem as he saw it from his vantage point was only a few feet above her lay a small sloping gravel section with no hand holds that made it impossible to climb over. She would have to move several feet to the left to move around this dangerous place that now hindered her progress.

"Move this way and you should be okay" he called loudly down to her.

"No, there's no holds on that side and only a few on the other. I don't think I can go either way. I'm sure I can climb over that gravel ledge above me, hopefully I can reach those rocks above."

"Don't try that!" John yelled, "That's far too risky. You might get part way up and then slide backwards and there's no place to hang unto."

"I'll be alright," came the reply, "I can scramble over that part fast and get a hand on the rock ledge above. It's not so very steep."

"No! Don't do it!" John's voice now had a note of deep concern. This maneuver was far too risky and her life was in serious jeopardy.

"Stay there and I"ll come over your way."

As he began to move sideways to get closer he watched in trepidation and a deep feeling of foreboding as Mary had already begun to try to climb over the outer edge of the gravel section. He stopped and watched as she seemed to have hesitated part way up the incline.

She had come to a spot where she could not move upwards or sideways as one foot kept slipping off a small point and had only a slight toe hold on the other. She had managed to get her upper body over some of the stony ledge but had only one hand hold to help her hang on.

With no place to put her fingers and toes and no way to move up she glanced wildly around hoping to see somewhere she could climb. Fear was beginning to overcome her and the one suspended foot had begun to shake while the only foot holding her was losing strength. Her one hand that clung to a small crevice was weakening and making things worse was the other hand could not find any hold.

Desperately she scanned all the indentations and holes where she might get some leverage. There was little or no chance now to get the rest of the way over this small sand-gravel incline she was suspended on. Time was running out if she found no way to move forward.

"What's wrong honey?" John had come across the face of the cliff and now was some twenty feet above her.

"I can't move," came the reply, "I don't know how long I can hang on with only one leg holding me."

"Stay strong babe and stay calm so you can control your body, I'll try to climb down and give you a hand. Just keep hanging on."

The dangers are well known among rock climbers who use no safeties. Often one slip can be the end of life but few consider this when free climbing. To come back down a steep wall is usually either impossible or nearly so as the climber cannot see the hand or foot holds below him.

John knew the difficulties involved in trying to come back down to give Mary a hand but without hesitation he began to descend carefully one foot after the other. His only thought was to get to the point where he could reach his loved one and help her over this hurdle. He had been in some precarious situations before and been fearful but for some reason this time his only thought was to save Mary from falling.

Looking down the steep cliff he could see her hanging on with one foot dangling in open space and far below the car was but a speck. Time seemed to stand still as he kept looking at his feet and the rock wall to find foot holds to support him.

"Hurry hon, I only have one hand holding me and one foot. My other leg is shaking and I have no place to put it." Mary's voice trailed off to a whisper.

John lowered his body to just above the gravel incline where he could look into her face. Fear of falling had taken over and now she was close to panic. He managed to turn sideways so he could reach down and hopefully be able to get a hold of her loose hand. Wedging one of his running shoes into a small slot a few inches above the slide of shale he bent down with one arm extended. His hand was still over a foot short of her outreached hand. Now what he wondered? If he put a foot on the fine gravel he would slide right into her.

As his brain raced all thought or concern for his own safety had evaporated and all he knew was he must save the love of his life.

"Here's what you got to do hon," he spoke softly to her. You have to reach way up to my hand and grab it with all your strength and then spring up unto the shale and keep moving using your hands and feet to scramble up beside me and then keep moving."

"I don't think I can do it," she replied, her voice cracking. "I'm shaking and really scared."

"You can do it sweetheart." John replied, "Once I have a grip on your hand I'll pull with all my might. If you slip or I don't have the strength to pull you up then we will both go together."

For a full minute she stalled as fear had paralyzed her. Indecision was etched across her face as she tried to summon the courage to make the attempt. Not often the average person has to make a decision that if they fail they will die but in this case she had to try as there was no other choice.

Mary looked up at her husband's face one last time in the hopes he had reconsidered this move and had come up with some other plan.

She could tell by his expression it had to be now or never. With a feeble gesture she reached upwards over the slide and saw John's hand close as he reached far down. He was on the tipping point of balance and could easily be pulled off his perch. With a slight spring up she slid her body on the fine pebbles while trying to find his hand. Suddenly she felt her right hand go into his and he gripped her with all he had and pulled while leaning back against the rock face. One of her legs was loose scratching for some foot hold and then both feet were scrambling frantically looking for leverage. To the right of John she could see a hold and grasped unto it while still clinging to him.

She managed to lay flat against the cliff for a moment as she found small footholds and was able to breathe more deeply as the adrenalin began to subside.

"Keep going darling, it won't take us long to reach the top now and it's not as steep above." he said to her while calming himself from the close encounter.

Once they recovered they continued up the cliff with Mary in the lead and in less than a half an hour were climbing over the edge of the escarpment. On the top was grass and weeds but the big hill was flat and fell away gradually to the backside where they could descend in relative safety compared to the rock face they had just come up.

The pair lay in the grass recovering from their close encounter with disaster. Both were very thankful they were still alive and inwardly each one promising to never do such a foolish stunt again. Little did they know how many more exciting adventures that lay ahead in their young lives.

Was there any repercussions from this afternoon climb you might ask? The answer is yes. Within a few days they both were scratching at the skin on their legs and arms from a bad case of poison ivy. They surmised the poisonous weed was growing where they had laid down to rest.

To finalize our little story it must be said that although they would be involved in many more outdoor activities this young couple gave up rock climbing for a past time and focused on more down to earth things that you may read about in other stories if you find time.

Several years later this couple was brought to the saving grace of Jesus Christ and now look back on those times knowing God had kept them for that day.

Written by John Gearey
January 2014

Mishap on Mijin Lake

Mijinemungshing Lake is situated in Lake Superior
Park some 30 miles south of the small town of
Wawa in the province of Ontario. The lake has two
long arms and several islands which add to the enhancement and
appeal for the outdoor enthusiast. Because of the large population
of lake trout and brook trout many come to enjoy this wilderness
spot for the reason of fishing.

Thirty men from a local church had planned to spend a
weekend on this picturesque lake and enjoy a retreat and some
R&R. Little could they know of the nearly tragic events that were
about to unfold.

The morning was sunny and cool as six men in the lead party
arrived on the shores of Mijin Lake. As the forerunners they would
paddle to the campsite and make preparations for the remainder of
the party that would arrive later in the day. Flo Labelle the man
who had volunteered as main cook and bottle washer began to load
the food supplies and cooking utensils into the waiting canoes.
Lake Superior Park was a wilderness park set aside for campers,
hikers and fishermen and did not allow motorized vehicles so he
was loading the canoes carefully as he had brought a great deal of
gear.

The gang of six headed down the lake paddling effortlessly
through the pale blue water with Flo the man considered to be the
most important sitting among a pile of cooking accessories, while
Tim his friend and main helper paddled in the stern.

Directly behind them came P.J. and Dan in a short Sportspal
canoe. P.J. a tall man, blessed with a little less hair than most which

often turned rosy red when subjected to the summer sun had a broad grin on his oval face. He had been looking forward to this trip with great anticipation. Still in his thirties he was strong and loved the outdoors and especially fishing. Dan was in the stern, another man somewhat overweight, short and stocky and nearing fifty years of age and loved hunting and fishing and telling tales of past adventures.

Bringing up the rear in another loaded canoe came Dave S. and Les. Both men enjoyed the time they could have with other men of like minded faith. Les was a man as well who when hair was handed out thought the Lord said "Do you want hair or do you want to share?".so he said I'll share and now has little hair.

P.J. sat tall in the bow of the front canoe and pointed to circles on the surface of the clear water that indicated rising trout. His heart began to beat faster as he grew eager to try a cast among the feeding fish. Dan continued to direct the canoe towards the island with the campsite while keeping an eye on his partner who often would dig deeply into the water with his paddle causing the canoe to dip dangerously to one side or the other.

"I've got a great idea P.J." chirped Dan.

"What's that Dan?"

"After we drop off all this gear and set up our tents let's portage over to Wabigoon Lake and fish for some brook trout. Here in this lake we'll probably catch only lakers."

"Sounds great to me old buddy, the sooner we unload the sooner we can get to the fun stuff." the big man in the front yelled over his shoulder.

The group of canoes were soon slipping up unto the gravel beach of an island that had been chosen for the camping spot. The pebble beach would accommodate several canoes and the area was large enough for all the tents.

Some of the men whisked the gear and boxes up to the site while others began to set up their tents. Flo was busy setting up tables and hanging tarps in the event of rain and making preparations for the evening meal for the large group of men that were coming later.

Others were busy pulling out their fishing rods and tackle and were in great haste to be out on the water in search of the elusive trout.

Dan finished the task of setting up his tent and looked over at his partner.

"You got your fishing gear ready?" he growled.

"Yup, sure do." came the reply.

"'Well lets get going, Wabigoon Lake is calling?

With a brief goodbye to their friends they were soon in their canoe and headed for the north arm of the large lake. A strong breeze had developed out of the west and a chop on the water was hitting them broadside. Dan worked his paddle to keep the canoe angled into the wind.

P.J. was in the bow and did not look forward to the long portage that lay ahead but was anxious to get in some quality fishing.

One hour later found the two men trolling and casting the shoreline of a lake some half mile in width and a little more in length. The wind was blowing briskly causing the canoe to rock from side to side making it difficult to travel up against the waves. Dan in the stern found it difficult to keep on a straight course and troll as well. Time was passing and they each managed to land a brook trout in spite of the windy condition. The long carry in had been tiring and now having to work at paddling the fishermen were becoming exhausted. They continued fishing close to shore but by late afternoon they knew the time had come to head back to camp. Neither man relished the thought of the long portage ahead. They landed at the start of the trail leading back to Mijin Lake and Dan hoisted the old canoe up on his shoulders and headed off towards the lake. P.J. followed behind panting under his load of gear and was soon sweating profusely. He perspired easily being a little overweight and out of shape and had begun to feel hunger pangs. They had not taken time to eat since breakfast hours ago. The wind seemed to diminish as they traveled down the trail and that was a blessing. He needed rest and some food and knew he was growing weaker as time went on. It would be good to be back at the camp slurping hot tea and gorging on some of Flo's famous supper meal.

"Wow, I"m getting bushed" Dan sang out as he put down the canoe for a rest.

"Yeah, me too" replied P.J. "We must be close to Mijin"

"Not far now, so let's get going." his partner commented as he lifted the canoe back on his shoulders and started down the trail.

As they drew closer to the big lake they could hear the wind howling through the tops of the trees. Both men were becoming concerned as they approached the shore. Great waves were pounding the shoreline and water was spraying over the big rocks as Dan set the canoe down to survey the situation. They were going to get wet and it would be difficult to get out unto the lake without taking on water.

The strong wind buffeted them as they pushed off shore paddling hard to keep from being thrown back against the boulders. Slowly they managed to get out of the small bay and into the wide expanse they needed to cross in order to make it to the large island and safety. However out here the waves had become swells and trying to paddle crosswise to the wind was extremely dangerous. The canoe had begun to take on water as the two exhausted men paddled with all their strength. They knew they were in deep trouble with the small craft. Dan tried to angle the canoe up against the wind as P.J. put all his strength into a paddle stroke. It was at this moment that time seemed to stand still for our two tired voyagers. They felt the canoe begin to tip and then suddenly they found themselves in the cold frigid waters of Mijin Lake.

A large wave hit Danny in the face, taking his breath away. He could hear a voice not far away.

"Danny, Danny, are you alright?" P.J. was screaming above the wind. Choking and sputtering Dan cried out to his friend. "I'm ok so far, how about you?"

P.J. was hanging onto the side of the canoe and treading water.

The waves washed over him and water went down his throat. How quickly they had ended up in the water. Thoughts raced through his mind as he wondered how long they could last in the freezing water and if anyone could see the difficulty they were in? Was this to be the final chapter of their lives? He had heard of others who had succumbed to the cold spring waters of the northern lakes and he knew the ice had melted on this lake very recently.

On the other end of the canoe Dan was holding unto the front gunwale of the canoe with one hand while trying to put on his life jacket with the other. After several unsuccessful attempts he became exhausted as he continued to tread water with his grip on the canoe growing weaker.

He was very cold. He could feel the icy fingers of the frigid water sinking into his inner being but could hear P.J.'s voice over the wind.

"Dan, do you see any canoes in sight?"

Somehow he didn't sound right.

"No, there's no one in sight." he hollered as loud as he could.

"I'm going to head for that small island over there." P.J. yelled back

"Stay with the canoe P.J., somebody will see us soon." Dan cried weakly as he took a wave in the face. It was too late. His friend had let go and was back peddling towards a small island some distance away. He was able to hear P.J.'s voice over the wind, "I can't last and I'm too cold. I have to get out of the water."

Dan knew he must hang onto the canoe as his strength was ebbing fast.

Their only hope was that someone would see them and come quickly.

His whole body was sluggish from being in the water for so long. His hands were slipping on the gunwale but he didn't seem to care any longer.

Turning his head slowly against the waves he thought he saw something up the lake. He tried to focus but was unable to. Hopefully some one was coming.

Perhaps he would not being going to heaven to-day if he could hang on a little longer.

Some distance away P.J. was struggling against the wind and waves. He could see a small island not far off but it was rocky with waves washing over it and would be wet and slippery. His arms didn't move well and his legs were numb. He tried to look back to see how Dan was doing but was unable to see him.

As the Pastor of the local assembly his heart broke as he thought of Dan succumbing to the elements.

"I think I've lost him," he muttered to himself with tears in his eyes.

Looking up the lake he saw a dark object.

Barry and Dave slowly approached in a tippy looking canoe.

"What happened John, you guys get too hot and decided to go for a swim?" chirped Dave.

"Go check out Dan," P.J. yelled to them. "I hope he's okay but I can't see him on the other side of the canoe."

"Are you going to be okay?" Barry asked.

"Yeah for a little while but I'm growing weaker." came the reply.

"Hang on John, others are coming." Dave yelled in the wind.

The two men headed for the overturned canoe which had been swept down the lake some distance away.

Nearing the swamped craft they could see Dan bobbing alongside desperately clutching the gunwale.

"Come on Dan let go and we"ll try to pull you into our canoe." yelled Barry as he tried to keep them from being hit broadside by the pounding waves. Dan let go and grasped the side of Barry's canoe but his strength failed and he almost capsized it when he tried to rest his upper body on the edge.

"I can't do it fellas." he gasped.

"Okay Dan, just hang on for a moment and we'll try to get you up on top of the thwart and get you inside." The attempt would be extremely risky.

Derek and Ron pulled up with their larger canoe and came

alongside. As they steadied the smaller canoe they knew how difficult this was going to be, but felt they could get him in if they worked together with Barry and Dave.

Moments later they managed to get the heavy man up half way and then with the waves crashing against the sides they pulled him into the bottom of their craft.

Dave and Barry began the paddle with their human cargo back to the campsite.

Ron and Derek now paddled towards P.J. and soon came up to him.

"Hang on John we could try to get you in the canoe." Barry yelled.

He could see the man was losing strength quickly.

"No we can't risk it chum, just throw me a rope and drag me back to camp. I think I have the strength to hang on." John gurgled in a shaky voice.

Another canoe had moved up alongside with Timo and Jerry who threw him a rope and began to tow him. Some distance down the lake yet another canoe was coming with Dave A. and John G. They had seen two red blobs in the distance and wondered what was going on. As they drew closer they could tell a serious mishap had occurred and asked how they could help. Someone asked them to retrieve Dan's empty canoe that was being swept quickly down the lake.

There was deep concern for P.J. and whether the long time in the water would cause his body to shut down from the cold. Everyone was praying that God would give him added strength in his hour of need. Timo kept talking to the big man hoping to keep him focused and alert. It was a long distance to tow a human through the cold spring water and not have him succumb.

The first canoe to arrive back at camp was the canoe with Danny in the bottom who was now shaking badly and was beginning to go into the final stages of hypothermia. Derek and Ron worked quickly to get him out of the canoe with the help of others. They took off his wet clothes and wrapped him up in a dry blanket and put him in his sleeping bag.

Flo Labelle the cook had boiled some water and made black tea which Dan tried to drink even as he shook uncontrollably. His hands hardly had the strength to hold the cup. Worry showed on the faces of the men gathered around as Flo piled more blankets on the man who had finally slipped deep inside his heavy down bag.

Timo and Jerry had finally arrived with Pastor John and helped him out of the water. Barely able to walk on his own he staggered up the small incline to the campsite and collapsed by his tent. Some of the men stripped his wet clothes off and helped him into his tent. Flo gave him a sip of tea and began to massage his upper body to restore blood circulation as John seemed to be slipping into a coma. He tried to talk but was incoherent and finally he began to fall asleep as Flo continued to work on his body.

Although it was suggested someone should add their body heat to the two men inside the sleeping bags no one volunteered to offer this much need warmth.

Everyone had deep concern that these men would recover but no one knew for certain what would transpire.

Flo and others continued to check on their patients during the course of the next two hours. Finally after one such visit they heard Dan snoring softly and shortly after they checked P.J. and he as well was resting comfortably. Flo conveyed this news to the group and there was a great sigh of relief. Their hopes were raised and they thanked God for His mercies and answered prayer.

A short time later Dan came out of his tent looking much better and no longer cold. He immediately headed for the large camp fire where most of the men were huddled and began to answer their many questions.

Flo had prepared broth and mooseburgers and other good food which Dan felt he could eat now that he was warm and in dry clothes.

The smell of cooking covered the area and the men were beginning to chow down on the food when P.J. came out of his tent.

A chorus of voices arose when the men around the fire discovered that he was out and walking around.

"You're looking a lot better big guy," someone sang out.

"How are you feeling John?" Allen asked

"I feel pretty good." came the reply. "What's that smell?"

"We're cooking moose burgers" Flo replied feeling much relieved that both men were now up and moving.

"Wow, am I ever hungry, I can't wait to try those moose burgers!" he cried.

"Be careful John. Don't eat more than one of those." Allen said behind him.

Allen had taken Pastor John on several fishing and hunting trips over the years and knew of his propensity to overdue at times.

Only a few minutes later on the edge of the firepit Johnny G. another fishing partner of P.J.'s saw him finishing one burger and had two more in his hand.

"What are you doing John, didn't we warn you not to eat too much right away.

Your body is still in shock and can't stand a lot of food for awhile."

"I can't help myself, I've got to eat. I'm starved!" P.J. retorted.

"Stop now my friend or you will be sick later." rasped his friend.

"This happened once to me when I was overtired and hungry and was I ever ill."

"It's too late John, I've already eaten 5 burgers." came the reply.

"I can't believe it, he must have inhaled them as it's only been a few minutes since he came out of the tent." John G. muttered to those close by.

As the evening grew darker the wind began to recede and the lake became languid. The sky was clearing and the moon was beginning to rise in the east.

The men were huddled around a roaring fire talking up a storm, chewing on sweets and drinking tea and feeling good now the emergency was over. A lot of tall stories were bouncing back and forth among the men as the night crept along. Soon many disappeared into their tents after the long day on the water.

Danny and P.J. with their stomachs full of food grew drowsy, said their good-nights and headed for their tents as well. Peace and calm settled over the campsite and only the lonesome cry of the loon could be heard from across the lake.

Midway through the night a loud rasping sound broke the stillness of the forest. Johnny G. woke with a start. He knew a loud noise had awakened him from a deep sleep. And then he heard the sound again somewhere within the campsite.

Someone was sick. Very sick. Most of the men began to wake up. The loud noise was coming from P.J.'s tent. The man was vomiting violently over and over again. A couple of the men went to his tent to check on him to see if they could do something to help. However no one in camp had medication to help his upset stomach.

He was retching terribly and often and was beginning to go into shock.

No one seemed to know what to do except wait for daylight and take him to the hospital. Talking among themselves they reasoned they could only keep him warm and try to keep him calm. The night dragged on.

P.J. continued to retch and shake and so a couple of the men stayed with him. Finally in the wee hours of early morning as the night began to turn to grey Allan got his canoe ready and helped John Trudeau and another man place the big man in the bottom of a larger canoe. Side by side they paddled down the lake to the landing. By now P.J. was very weak and could barely make it from the canoe to John T.'s car.

The three men carried and dragged him with great difficulty and finally deposited him in the back seat where he lay moaning. With great concern they said goodbye to John T. as he sped out on the dusty road that led to the highway south to Sault Ste Marie and the hospital some hundred miles away.

As we conclude this tale of near disaster on a windy lake and the sickness that followed we wish to put all at ease. John Trudeau drove as quickly as allowed to the hospital with his patient and the doctors were able help P.J. recover though he remained ill for some time.

The other men all hoped that lessons were learned from this unusual weekend on Mijin Lake. Danny did recover fully and went back to his usual pursuit of adventure in the north.

There are still some questions that will always remain. ie How many moose burgers does it take to make a man ill?

And more importantly how did two men survive so long in the cold frigid waters of Mijin Lake in May? Survival time is usually quite short and body temperatures drop rapidly in a few minutes. Some call it amazing but most call it a miracle.

We know God answered the prayers of the men that day as they cried out for help.

The End

Written by John Gearey

Wilderness Camp

Three Amigos and One Bull Moose

Many years ago there were three amigo's who decided they would like to hunt the great monarch of the north, the large and majestic moose. Now in those days there were many moose that roamed the northern hinterland not far from where the three young friends lived, and these three friends had what some call moose fever. They each had an overwhelming desire to hunt down and shoot the biggest bull moose with the biggest rack ever known to man.

Should you not enjoy the reading of a story of the murder of a moose then perhaps you should set aside this gruesome tale and move to the next story soon to come. However it is my hope there are a few who might revel in the telling of an excursion into Lake Superior Park in search of one of the largest animals in the wilds of North America.

It all began on a beautiful autumn day in late September, one week before the opening day of the moose slaughter, excuse me, I mean the moose hunt. In those years so long past the tag system had only begun and almost every one could attain a tag for an adult moose in the Superior Park area. And so it was that our three stalwart companions had drawn a bull moose tag which was what they desired.

One week before the opening day of moose season Dave and John, two of intrepid trio pulled into a gravel pit on the east side of the highway that passed through the Park. The purpose of driving a hundred miles from home was to check out the area they planned to hunt and to line up the sights of a brand new Remington automatic rifle that Dave had recently purchased. Now here was a mighty proud man of a mighty fine gun.

It was very expensive and very good to look at (I speak of the gun of course) unless his wife was telling the story. Well polished and never used it was a sight to behold. John his buddy set up the targets so they could site in their weapons. The gravel pit was situated close to the Baldhead River a small river running east to west and entered Lake Superior a few miles away. John pulled out his 30.06 Remington carbine with a 1906 date stamped on the barrel. His Dad had given him this short heavy rifle as a gift after using it for nearly a half a century of hunting mule deer in the south west U.S. (I may be off by a few years). This particular gun had a kick that would equal a .458 elephant gun. The previous year John had shot his first moose. He had shot the animal from a small canoe and the recoil from the gun had almost sent him and his partner into the freezing November water. The calf had been standing on the shore of a small stream and took the lead behind the ear and fell dead on the spot. His shoulder had taken days to recover from the recoil but here he was ready to bang off several shots in target practice so he could be sure of dropping a huge bull moose but not sure if his shoulder would be back in shape in time for next weeks hunt.

And so they fired away at the big sheets of paper lined up on the opposite side of the gravel pit. Dave with his big new 9 power scope and John with his broken peep site. Dave with his great eyesight and big scope did well at 75 yards and John did well at 10 yards and so finally after firing off several hundred rounds they deemed themselves ready for the hunt.

Desperate would be the plight of the noble bull moose if these two ever crossed his path. Truly this would be a hunt to remember, one blind guide and one over zealous novice. And let us not forget the third member of our little party of moose hunters. Their good friend Rick, who was strong, resilient and brave at home preparing for the following week's hunt. His trusty 30-30 sat in the corner waiting for action. How long you ask? Someone had suggested before the War of 1812 which of course is absurd. More likely before the Great War.

However here was another hunter with great hopes of bringing down a gigantic moose with a rack that spanned at least six feet. And so the little gun sat patiently waiting for this years outing.

Now that Dave and John had convinced themselves they could hit a running target at a thousand yards they decided to hike up an old logging road behind the gravel pit to search out moose sign. Slinging their shotguns over their shoulders off they went in search of tracks and perhaps bag a grouse or two.

The autumn sun had begun to sink rapidly when the two tired hunters arrived back at their vehicle with no grouse and no more enlightened of the moose than when they had begun three hours earlier.

The next Friday was the day before moose season opened. John was at the wheel of his old Dodge truck heading north towards Lake Superior Park. Beside him sat his two friends Dave and Rick, their gear all piled in the back of the beat up 4X4. This vehicle was indeed a sight to behold as it rumbled down the highway with its many rusty parts and huge dents covering the majority of the fenders and doors.

Truly these three intrepid amigos were going on a wing and a prayer of ever arriving at their destination, a campground that lay due south of the town of Wawa.

As they entered the south boundary of the Park the trio kept a watchful eye for moose that might be browsing near the road. Kinney Lake loomed on their right and reminded them of a scene on a postcard of years past. Shortly they saw the road to Mash Lake on the right and Gargantua road on the left. John jammed on the brakes as they neared the bridge that crossed the Baldhead

River.

"This is where we target practiced last week" he told Rick as the truck slowed to a crawl.

Suddenly Rick pointed to a small stand of trees close to the highway on the right.

"Look fellas, do you see that?" John skidded the truck to a stop on the gravel shoulder. "There goes one" Dave yelled. John was peering into the scrub brush when he saw a cow moose standing nonchalantly watching them. Almost immediately another moose ran up to join the first one.

"I can see more of them." Rick sang out. "There is three cows standing together among the thicket of those small yellow birches".

Embracing the moment of excitement John with his usual sense of optimism muttered, "Now that we've seen moose today what's the chance of seeing more to-morrow. "

His friends gave him a withering look and asked him to pull down into the gravel pit a few feet ahead. The moose had begun to move and soon slid into oblivion among the trees as they watched intently. Then the three men piled out of the truck and began to scout around for more sign, hoping to find the tracks of a bull moose, or even better to see one. Visions of the great beast of the north stirred their minds as they ran around the area. With hearts pumping and great hope urging them on they searched diligently but no more was seen of the moose. Finally they agreed to go on to Rabbit Blanket campground where they would stay for the week.

The next morning came with a light drizzle and a dull, dreary looking sky. The first ray of light began to creep into the eastern sky as Dave crawled out of his sleeping bag. They had put up a large green canvas tent the night before but without heat in the tent the moisture hung heavy.

"Rise and shine boys" Dave yelled "Let's go get some moose".

His two buddies stirred, and with some mumbling and grumbling managed to make it out of the tent. By now the rain was coming down harder as the group stood under a blue tarp they had hastily erected the night before. They sipped hot coffee and chewed on some cold toast and hard eggs that Rick had prepared on a Coleman Stove. The large tarp reached from the back of the truck to the front of the tent and helped keep them dry.

With out a doubt this would be a trip to be remembered. Damp,chilly and miserable with little hope of finding a moose they donned their rain gear.

Dave and John wore cheap rain suits that would probably wet through quickly once they entered the bush. However here they were, ready to hunt and no amount of rain would deter them from the morning hunt. Neither wet, nor cold nor possibility of pneumonia. All such thoughts were put aside as they loaded their gear consisting of axes, saws, come-a-longs and ropes in the back of the battered truck.

Each one took time to check his rifle and ammo so they would be ready to fire in the event that there was a male moose dumb enough to be out walking around on a day like this.

"Let me off at Otter Lake" Rick sang out as he climbed into the passenger seat. "I'll walk down the road and check for sign."

"Yeah, I'll go with you" Dave added.

"Alright fellas, I'll drop you off so you can go play in the rain and I'll head down to the Gami road and sit in my nice dry truck and wait for the moose to come out. Have fun!" and away he drove.

John did not feel like hiking around in the heavy rain and knew of a great spot to park where he could overlook a branch of the Baldhead River which ran south into Otter Lake. Two years earlier a hunter he knew had shot a moose close by.

A short drive brought him to the road and he parked on a rise that gave him a full view of the area. How nice it was to sit in a dry truck with a heater and ponder on the things of the world while his buddies went tromping around on a muddy road in the pouring rain. He well knew that moose in general do not move a lot when it is raining but one never can tell. Hope swells strong in the heart of the mighty moose hunter.

Meanwhile on the Otter Lake road Rick and Dave were slowly making their way east while watching carefully along the sides of the road. Otter Lake area had always been a mecca for moose through the years and should remain so for a long time.

"Look at the size of that hoof print", Rick cried out. He was eager to find a moose with a massive rack that would adorn his rec room wall back home.

"There must have been a whole herd that passed through here last night", sang out Dave excitedly.

Tracks were everywhere in the sandy parts of the road. The men continued down the trail that veered around the end of Otter Lake and headed eastward. The rain continued to beat down as they peered into the surrounding brush on either side. Dave felt cool water running down inside his cotton T-shirt. Somehow his rain gear was letting in moisture and he could feel the dampness creeping around his chest. Visibility was good as he observed the hardwoods on the hillsides. There were only a few reds and oranges left with a touch of yellow. He should be able to see movement even on this dismal day. The two climbed a small hill near the road which allowed them to look far below to a distant valley. A stand of yellow tamarack stood out sharply against the green conifers on a nearby ridge. "Now there's a place for moose to bed down." he murmured, "maybe we should head down into the valley?"

"It's too wet and slippery to go pushing our way down that hill, Dave." Rick commented. "Let's head back towards the main road and see if that John fella has found anything."

The two bedraggled men, their face and hands wet and cold and their guns in the same condition turned and began to make their way up the soggy, water filled road hoping their buddy would be waiting for them in a dry truck.

Meanwhile John had suddenly sat up and looked down in a thicket of scrub elders near the stream. He thought he had seen movement or was that just wishful thinking? He had been sitting here on this knoll overlooking a small branch of the Baldhead for over two hours and maybe, just maybe there was an animal coming up unto the road. The drizzle had continued steadily and would make it miserable to go scouting around.

Waiting patiently for movement it seemed as if whatever was down there had decided to stay put. Looking at his watch he realized he should be heading down the main road to pick up his two friends who would be well soaked by now and ready for a hot drink.

As he pulled the old power wagon out unto the road he could see in the distance two water sogged individuals heading his way. He drove slowly toward them wondering how they had managed to stay out that long in this miserable weather. They gave him a look of disdain as he stopped the truck beside them.

"Jump in fellas and we'll go get a hot drink and dry clothes", he chortled.

"Sure Johnny, that's a good idea, you really got wet this morning didn't you?" rasped Dave who could see his friend was dry as a bone.

John grunted with a smile on his face as he knew how warm and dry he had stayed. After arriving back at camp and making hot drinks and snacks they sat around the campfire pondering their next move. The fearless trio knew they must venture forth that evening for that would be a likely time for their massive moose to show itself. Looking overhead as they fed themselves they could see small breaks in the grey clouds. A slight breeze had come up and was pushing clouds around as the afternoon wore on. In a short time the skies began to brighten and then a ray of sunlight shone through. Jumping off his seat Rick yelled. "Hey guys look at the sun, let's go hunting."

Dave responded quickly by grabbing his gun and heading for the vehicle.

"Come on John my man, we're going to kill a moose to-night."

Always the optimist thought John but still he felt good about going. One never knew what might happen.

With less than two hours of daylight left they motored down the road.

"Keep your eyes peeled fellas we might see one." Rick pointed along the edge.

"Let's head up to where we saw the three cows last night" John replied. The other two agreed and they soon pulled into the lane leading to the Baldhead gravel pit. With great anticipation they sat in the truck surveying the area and watching for movement. Quietly they slipped out of the vehicle and split up. Dave headed up the trail behind the gravel pit while John and Rick went up on the bridge on the highway that crossed over the river. They planned to head up the small river to scout for sign.

Richard dropped down from the gravel shoulder of the big road cradling his trusty 30-30. John followed close behind grasping his snub nosed shoulder whacking 30:06 in one hand and separating the brush with the other.

The shadows were growing longer and the sun was dropping quickly behind the hills and each man knew they didn't have long before the forest would be dark. Rick moved cautiously forward following a dim trail made by a large animal. The trail was crowded with saplings and alders that hindered his view.

He stopped and motioned John forward. In a whisper he said "See that!"

His friend moved quietly forward with eagerness. The ground was wet and soggy and the trees were dripping from the rain. A spray of cold water from one of the branches hit him in the face. As he peered ahead he could see a small clearing.

"Holy smokes!" he exclaimed.

Surrounding them was evidence of where a bull moose had scraped the trees and tore up the whole area in rut.

"Look Johnny, he must be huge, he's broken off alders higher than we can reach."

"Yeah and he must have been here yesterday or to-day as this all looks fresh."

As the pair scouted around they could see where the ground was tore up all over with sign of more than one moose. However they did not see or hear a sound in the bush. Sadly they knew the big moose had moved on and so with tempered hearts they turned to head back up the trail.

Their excitement at finding all the sign was abating and well did they know the odds of ever seeing him were slim.

"Boom!" the sound came from across the river.

Rick and John came to an abrupt halt and listened intently.

"Did you hear that?" Rick softly voiced his inquiry.

"Boom!" There it was again and it sounded close.

The two looked at each other and John yelled "Let's get over there, Dave has shot a moose!"

Plunging through the wet brush the excited pair ran as fast as they could, up unto the highway, down the road past the truck and around the gravel pit. Still no sign of Dave or a moose.

"Let's head up the old logging road" puffed John as he tried to catch his breath.

They slowed to a walk and kept a look-out hoping to see their friend or a moose. Darkness was descending rapidly as the sun dropped from sight. And then down the road they saw Dave running towards them.

"I got him! I got him!" Dave yelled out between breaths. With bulging eyes and red face he barely was able to gasp out the words.

"He's just around the corner, I'll show you."

The three hurried back down the trail where Dave had come.

"How big is he?" Rick wanted to know. How much he wished he could have been the one doing the shooting.

"He's big, he is really, really big Rick and he's got a gigantic rack." Dave responded.

Around the corner of the road they swept eager to see this monstrous animal they had all hoped to shoot.

"Where is he?" asked John as they approached the site.

"Well, I shot him in the brisket as he came out on the road, and you can see by the skid marks in the mud where he went down and then got up again. Wow was he big, but I tried to get another shot but my gun jammed but finally I was able to shoot at him again as he headed into the bush. I remember thinking as I fired, is this all there is to moose hunting? Walk down a road and a moose appears a few feet away?"

As mentioned earlier this was the first time for Dave to go moose hunting and the first time he had ever used his brand new rifle. What a moment for this killing machine.

"He could not have gone far with a bullet in him". said Rick always the voice of reason.

And so with twilight upon them, three of the world's finest trackers went charging about trying to follow spatters of blood left by the wounded animal.

Through the brush they walked, bent over peering at the wet leaves and branches hoping to find signs of the fleeing moose. Occasionally one of them would sing out when they saw a spatter of blood. The frantic gang of hunters stayed on the trail till the falling darkness made it almost impossible to see more than ten feet ahead.

Rick was ahead when he yelled out "I lost the trail, it's too dark."

"We'd better get back to the truck, as fast as we can" John commented.

They began to head towards the old logging road, Dave, his head bent low with a sad heart hating the thought of going back to camp and leaving a dying animal in the bush.

Each one fell into a pensive mood as the intense excitement of the chase faded and they thought of how they might find this grand old moose? What a shame to have him suffer during the night. Many other thoughts invaded their unsettled minds as they traveled back to camp. In the truck Dave rambled on about seeing the moose come out and how he stopped to look at him and how the great animal skidded after being shot and how it recovered so quickly and ran away leaving the hunter shaking like a leaf.

John hoped they would find the big bull in the morning and find his Puma knife he had lost while rushing about in the bush. However he knew there was little hope of finding either.

During the night the men slept little. Dave tossed and turned with visions of his lost moose. Needless to say they were anxious and eager to be on the trail the following morning.

The day began crisp and cool with the sun coming up over the tree tops as the three amigos headed back to retrace their steps from the night before.

"Let's spread out and meet back here in two hours." suggested Rick.

Each went his separate way scouring the bush, looking for sign, blood or tracks or broken branches. For two hours they diligently searched.

John arrived back on the road first and was staring at the marks left by the wounded moose from the night before when Dave came up to him.

"I haven't found a sign of that moose, Johnny. Have you had any luck?" he asked hopefully.

"No" John responded, "I could not find the moose or my knife."

From behind them they could hear Rick coming through the bush. As he arrived the question was on their lips. "Any luck pal?"

"No" he replied, "I've searched everywhere." He could see the long faces on his friends.

The three men stood looking forlornly at each other. What a sad day for the three great white hunters. There would be no celebration to-night or forever about this hunt.

As Dave and John turned slowly to make their way back down the trail Rick spoke again.

"Actually guys I'm only kidding, I found him." Rick's well tanned face broke into a huge grin.

"Really?" Dave could barely contain himself as he tried to believe his chum's words.

"Where is he?" asked John

"Well guys, he's in that big pond just this side of the gravel pit. I had almost given up when I remembered someone saying that a wounded moose will always head for the nearest water, so I kept going towards the gravel pit. As I neared the shoreline of the little pond I could see what looked like the branches of a tree sticking up out of the water, and so I walked around to take a closer look and sure enough there was a large set of moose racks sticking out of the water. I would have missed him had I not seen the rack because the rest of him was under water."

Suddenly the realization that the lost moose was found hit Dave like a thunderbolt. He jumped with joy, and shook Rick's hand and thanked him and then shook John's hand in celebration. Congratulations flowed and Dave was like a new man with a great burden taken off him. With high anticipation Dave and John followed Rick through the bush towards the spot he had found the animal. In only a few moments the three sturdy amigo's stood on the shoreline of the small pond gazing at the submerged animal in the shallow water.

At this moment of time we must ask was it luck that brought Rick to the pond and was it simply by chance he even thought of heading in that direction? And how come Rick decided to check out what appeared to be the branches of a fallen tree protruding from the water? Many questions still remain unanswered unless you believe God in his kindness led Rick to the spot and God's goodness prevailed.

After finding the huge animal they now had the ponderous task of getting the moose out of the water, quartering it and hauling it back to camp.

The work carried on through the day and by midnight the men were back at camp with their prize.

The story of the packing out of the huge moose head with the great rack attached, and the four large quarters would be told many times in the years ahead. How they winched the great beast out of the water after pulling it across the pond behind the canoe and all the sweating and striving that went on that stretched the three amigo's to the point of exhaustion is a story by itself.

How Johnny's little canoe carried each piece precariously

across the expanse of water in the gravel pit. And how in the dark with only one small light to guide them they managed to carry the meat and head and rack and load them into the back of the vehicle will all be part of what remains in the memory of the three amigos.

As we close this tale of excitement, and of sadness turned to joy we happily wish to tell you that the huge head and rack of this noble monarch hangs proudly in the office of Dave, barrister, solicitor and remarkable hunter. And now every morning when he enters his office Dave quietly says to the beast, "Good Morning Morley"

For that is his name forever. MORLEY THE MOOSE.

The End

Written by John Gearey

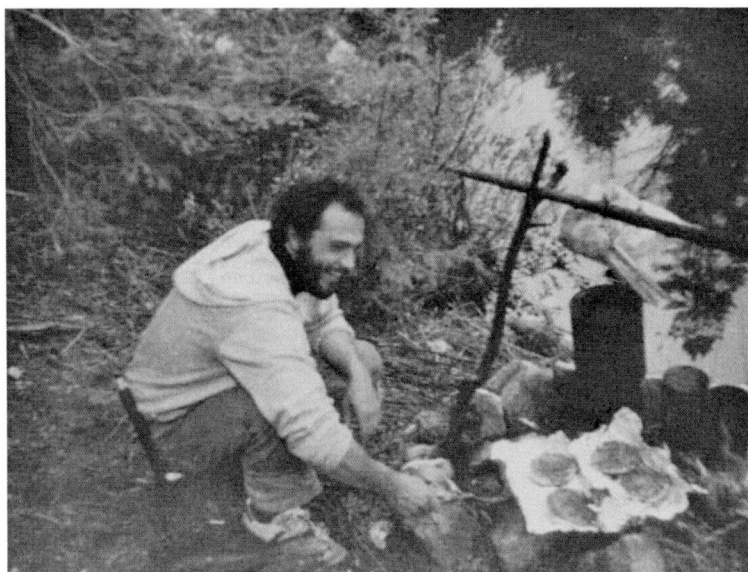

Chico Cooking

Challenging the Wild Aubinidong

One hundred years ago Teddy Roosevelt, the former President of the United States was persuaded to challenge an unexplored river nicknamed the "The River of Doubt" located in the Brazilian jungle. Roosevelt who was in his mid fifties nearly lost his life and lived only a few short years after this harrowing experience.

Through the last two hundred years, hundreds of wild rivers have been run by all kinds of adventure seeking folks, from courier de bois to modern day kayak enthusiasts. From the famous running of the Colorado River by Powell in the 1800's to portions of other wild rivers through out the world men and women have risked their lives for the pure enjoyment and thrill of running an unknown river.

This story began on a sunny warm June morning in the mid seventies of the past century. Four young men had decided to challenge a river called the Aubinidong, a wild untamed river with few portages and a large number of rapids and waterfalls. Ted Thompson, one of Canada's Group of Seven painter's had run the river in the early 1900's and flipped over in a rapids losing most of his sketches.

Without much planning or foresight the four friends had made preparations for a long days run. Unable to locate any detailed maps they felt confident they had the necessary skill to survive the adventure. Youth has a way of overlooking the difficulties and dangers that older folks would take far more seriously.

Daylight was advancing rapidly over Gong Lake as two canoes slipped silently through the still waters heading for the creek that fed into the Aubinidong River.

Richard and his cousin Dave paddled a 14 foot fiberglass canoe made by Oscar a local canoe maker. Their friends Chico and John were in another Oscar canoe, a sixteen footer that weighted ninety pounds with a forty inch beam. Both canoes were sturdy but difficult to maneuver in fast water which did not seem to concern any of the stalwarts. They looked forward to running wild rapids and catching tasty trout. Little did they appreciate what lay ahead.

"How long a portage is it from the lake to the river?" asked Dave as the two canoes drew close together. He was on summer vacation after one year of law school and looked forward to the wilderness trip. After a long hard year at school this would be just what he needed to unwind.

"The map seemed to indicate at least a half a mile." chirped Chico from the bow of the larger canoe. "However these streams are sometimes deep enough in the spring to paddle through." Chico was a twenty one year old of medium stature and possessed athletic agility and strength and had taken to this type of outdoor adventure with great enthusiasm.

"Let's hope so." grunted Rick as he dipped his paddle deep into the water. A well muscled man with strong resolve he looked forward to an exciting day on the water.

A pair of loons nervously watched the two canoes from a short distance, their checkered backs glistening in the morning sun. The foreign invaders from the city slowed to watch one of the loons do a short vibrant tail stand and flap its wings furiously in a show for his mate.

"There it is, a little to the left," Chico pointed to an opening to a small winding creek a short distance ahead. Tall golden wands of marsh grass waved leisurely in the light breeze along the swampy shoreline as the waterway narrowed dramatically. The men moved slowly into shallower water watching for sunken logs and dead falls. They soon found themselves shoving their paddles deep into a dark colored muck, pushing with all their strength to keep the canoes moving forward. However it was not long before the tiny stream turned into a trickle of water and they were obliged to crawl out of the canoes, stepping gently on the boggy surface that surrounded them. Carefully they pulled their craft forward slipping and sliding on the muddy wet sides of the almost indistinguishable creek.

After a great deal of pushing and pulling and a lot of grouching by them all, Dave suddenly yelled back to his comrades.

"I think I see water ahead.' and with a burst of energy he charged forward through the tangle of myrica bushes. Within minutes he was standing on the shores of a small narrow river guarded by tightly woven evergreens.

The long difficult journey through the deep and boggy marsh that separated Gong Creek from the river Aubinidong was at last over. The four comrades were tired but ready to take on the challenge that lay ahead with unknown rapids, waterfalls and countless submerged rocks that waited to rip out the bottom of their canoes.

Quickly they pushed off shore and headed into the current with Rick and Dave pulling into the lead eager to find what lay around the next bend of the river.

"Look to your left guys!" sang out John the oldest of the group. "There's the Nashinagani River."

All eyes turned to catch a glimpse of a small fast flowing river that entered the Aubinidong from the northeast.

"I sure wish we had time to go up that river and try the trout fishing." he thought to himself as he wistfully watched it disappear behind him.

Soon their speed began to increase, and as they rounded a sharp curve they could hear the sound of a much larger rapids.

Dave looked back at his partner. "What do you think Rick, should we stop and have a look to see how big those rapids are?"

"No, I can see them and they're not bad at all," he replied. "Wish we had some detailed maps of the river." The pair sped through the light set of rapids with the second canoe hard behind them.

With a yell of exhilaration Chico voiced his excitement and

his readiness to get to the next set.

Cedar and spruce trees crowded the river banks as the two canoes whisked by in the fast moving water.

"Stop! Stop!" Dave suddenly bellowed from the bow of the front canoe. He could hear the sound of approaching rapids and they sounded much louder than the last set they had run.

Richard began to back paddle as hard as he could. The loud noise ahead was the unmistakable roar of a waterfall or at the very least a plunging chute.

"Let's find a spot to land on this side." Dave called out nervously as he could see mist rising off the water a couple of hundred feet ahead.

They swung their canoe into a small cove with slower moving water and espied a small opening under the overhanging boughs of a large white pine. Quickly they drove the canoe up unto a dry patch of land. John and Chico came up beside them grabbing the overhanging branches to keep from being pulled downstream.

"Let's go see what all the racket is about," said Rick as he walked about staring ahead. "Ah, here's a foot path but it's not very good." He hurried forward down a faint, steep trail.

The others followed and could see through the trees the river being forced into a narrow chute of granite rock, crashing several feet down. Foaming white spray covered the area and made for a spectacular view but impossible to navigate.

The decision to portage around the first half of the falls was not difficult but they decided to run the last half which included a two lip waterfall that ended in a swirling black pool at the bottom.

Rick and Dave carried their craft over the steep rocky trail and entered the water just above the small falls. Within seconds the swift current caught them and hurled them inexorably towards the first lip. Dave with a scream was sent out and over first and then they plunged down into a pool above the second falls which was the higher of the two. Time for only a strong paddle stroke and they were swept over the lip and dropped ten feet to the swirling water below.

Intoxicated with adrenalin the two maneuvered their craft to shore while filling the air with hoots and yells.

"Come on guys, you can do it." Dave yelled back to the other two standing on shore above the falls who had watched apprehensively as the smaller canoe had sped ahead and dropped from sight. Much relieved their comrades were safe it was now their turn.

"Are you ready chum?" asked John nervously looking at Chico.

"I think so, but it sure looks tricky," came the reply. He felt somewhat uneasy and he could tell Johnny was as well. Their canoe was a sixteen foot heavyweight that would not respond well in fast water. With a forty inch beam and three keels the beast belonged on a lake not in a fast narrow river. But here they were and try they must and so without another word they climbed aboard and pushed off shore.

Digging their paddles deep they flew towards the waiting falls. As they reached the brink of the first falls Chico screamed over the roar of the water.

"Watch the rock John! We're too close!" Looming to their left a huge pointed rock jutted far out over the lip, eye level with Chico. Disaster seemed imminent as they headed straight for the obstacle.

Chico reefed on his paddle with a strong draw stroke bringing the bow of the canoe to the right missing the pointed rock by inches. John in the stern struggled to straighten the canoe as they came to the drop off sideways and then he watched as if in slow motion the canoe capsize and sail over the first drop. The canoe and the men were sent crashing down into the cold water into the small pool below. The force of the water swept the big canoe over the next falls with the two men behind coming feet first.

John felt the cold water envelope him and then a moment of weightlessness before he felt extreme pain in one of his legs as he crashed unto the submerged rocks at the bottom of the last falls. He came up gasping for air while looking around for his comrade.

Dave waded out in the swift, shallow water and grabbed the

empty canoe as it headed down the river. Meanwhile Chico had managed to pull himself up on shore, wet but not hurt. Rick was standing on the shoreline casting out in the river trying to retrieve a leather hat that belonged to John.

"I'll get your hat!" he yelled to his friend who was struggling to get to shore.

"Great friend," thought John, "I could have a broken leg and be drowning and he's going to save my precious hat."

However, he was soon able to drag himself up on the slippery rocks on shore and begin to strip off his wet pants so he could look at his banged up knee.

"Are you okay?" asked Rick bringing the bedraggled leather hat over to him.

John sat on a flat rock rubbing his knee hoping the pain would subside.

"Yeah, thanks, I think this leg will work alright."

Chico had taken off his shirt and was wringing it out while watching Dave in the distance trying to retrieve the floating paddles as they headed downstream. He had already emptied the water out of the retrieved canoe and sat it upright. The fishing rods and small packs were still inside tied to the thwarts.

"Well boys you're a little wet," Dave said with a laugh as he approached with the paddles.

"Invigorating," Chico replied with a twinkle in his eye. "Whatever happened back there Johnny?" As he looked over at his friend who was still working on his knee.

"I couldn't get the stern to come around in time, that's all," he murmured with an air of exasperation. "We just couldn't pull it off that's all."

"Let's get going fellas." Rick's voice boomed as he headed for his canoe. "We've a long way to go." Dave jumped in the bow and they slid their craft into the swirling water and with one last look at their two soggy chums they headed downstream.

The other two were not long in following and looking ahead to see what awaited them next. As they softly paddled forward the sun began to dry their clothes and bring their body temperatures back to normal after the icy encounter with the river.

Mile after mile slipped by as the canoeists navigated the many riffles and boulder strewn rapids the river put in their path. As Rick and Dave rounded one of the many bends of the river they could see a long stretch of rapids filled with large rocks, many of them showing above water. As they drew closer Dave turned to look at his partner. "Should we try to get through that mess?"

"Sure let's give it a try" Rick responded. He hated lining the canoe along the rocky shoreline as they had been forced to do several times already. Often they had stumbled or bruised their feet and legs on the slippery rocks as they waded downstream. Behind them their friends could see the protruding rocks in the upcoming swifts.

"Let's go ashore Cheek and line this tub through that mess of rocks." John suggested.

"Sounds like a good idea to me. We could never make it between some of those boulders."

The two pulled their craft towards the nearest shore. A hundred yards ahead Rick and Dave had entered the swifts and were feverishly paddling trying to avoid the mass of rocks in their path.

"Whack, smack!" the canoe rammed into a huge boulder head on and then bounced off as Rick in the stern tried to keep it straight.

"Hang on, here we go!" yelled Dave as the canoe rattled off another dark rock then struck a barely visible obstruction under the water. They careened sideways as the men slashed the water frantically trying to keep the canoe upright.

"Crrr-runch", a sickening sound from under the canoe told them they had made contact with a hard sharp rock that probably had done severe damage.

"Hold on Dave," screamed Rick, "We're going to make it. I see deeper water ahead."

The battered craft wobbled and then short forward through

a small opening scraping the sides on two boulders. More large rocks came out of seemingly nowhere and they found themselves vaulted into a series of waves and being swept along at a great speed past the rocks.

"Left! Left!" Dave shouted as loud as he could as a huge rock loomed on his right. Missing it by inches he realized they were in serious trouble and could spill at any time.

He frantically tried to keep his paddle in the water and watch for hidden boulders. And then came a loud cracking noise as Rick desperately tried to keep the canoe from tipping. The water around them was dark and ominous and hid many unseen enemies below the surface that awaited to tear the bottom of the canoe open.

Suddenly the canoe rode up on the side of a smooth looking boulder that stood well above the water.

"Look out!" roared Dave as he clutched the gunwale of the canoe as it rose high in the air and then abruptly flung its two occupants into the cold swirling water of the wild river.

Richard, a strong swimmer came up out of the water with a lunge and grabbed the back of the canoe as they swept through the boulder infested river. On the opposite shore some distance behind John and Chico watched helplessly at this turn of events.

"We can't get over there to help them." Chico said with frustration.

"I can't see Dave, where is he?" John asked worriedly.

They watched Rick struggling to get the small craft to shore in the fast moving water. He was yelling but couldn't see his partner as he looked wildly around. As they neared the shore, the canoe smashed against another rock and then stalled.

A wave of panic swept over Rick and then he dived under the canoe in a desperate attempt to locate his lost cousin.

Coming up between the gunwales under the canoe he found Dave choking and kicking trying to disengage himself from the bobbing weight that held him down.

As Rick reached to grab him he suddenly sunk out of sight in the water below. With a great burst of strength Rick heaved the canoe up and sideways while grabbing Dave's arm as he came up gasping for air. The two struggled towards shore stumbling and slipping on the rocks below. Finally with their energy almost gone they managed to drag the craft into a slow eddy and haul themselves up unto a shallow embankment. With a wave of his hand Rick signaled to his friends that they were alright.

Chico and John feeling much relieved began to carefully line their canoe down through the myriad of rocks that impeded their way. The surging water threatened to upend them with each step. John suddenly fell forward scraping his shin on a sharp rock as his injured knee gave way but Chico steadied the canoe as his friend pulled himself up and began to move carefully forward on the slippery moss covered rocks below.

Meanwhile a hundred yards ahead their two soaked friends had emptied the water out of their canoe and prepared to launch back into the swirling mass.

"You guys okay" Chico yelled ahead to the two men.

"Yeah, we're fine." came the faint reply as they swung out from shore and headed back into the rapids.

John and Chico continued to line their craft through the treacherous area as they watched the other two forge ahead.

As the first canoe approached quieter water Dave turned slightly to look back at his cousin. "Thanks old buddy for the hand back there." he blurped with a small choking sound in his voice.

"You're welcome chum." Rick replied. "We have to take care of each other sometimes."

He was eyeballing the damage to the bottom and side of the canoe.

"We've smashed her up pretty good, wouldn't you say?" Dave remarked with a touch of concern in his voice.

"In more than one place." Rick responded, "Many more hits like those and we'll be hiking out." He watched as water seeped through some cracks along the bottom.

In a few minutes their two partners pulled up beside them

wearing big smiles.

"What are you two grinning at?" Dave asked with a note of agitation.

"Keep going like that and you'll be taking back Oscar's canoe in pieces." quipped John with a short laugh.

"We'll probably have to buy it off him anyway." Rick commented.

Pushing off from the gravel shore the four men kept the two canoes side by side for a long stretch of peaceful water.

"I wonder how far to the next set of falls?" asked Chico.

"Who knows, but hopefully there's some fish in the pools below it," his friend replied.

The sun had moved higher in the sky as they moved downstream through more riffles and light rapids.

"Let's stop and have a bite to eat guys, I'm starving." Dave yelled.

Rick stopped paddling and pulled out a granola bar and began gnawing away on it as the others came alongside.

"Do you hear that?" Dave asked putting his hand to his ear. They all went silent. Far in the distance they could hear a distinct rumbling noise.

"Let's paddle a little further." he volunteered. Coming around the next bend they could feel the river growing swifter and hear the muffled roar of a large waterfall.

"Yeah, that's the first of the big falls alright." whispered John. "Let's see how close we can get before hauling out."

They moved quickly past tightly knit trees that hugged the rugged shoreline. There seemed to be little chance of finding a spot big enough to land. The sound of roaring falls grew louder and louder. They were hoping to see some place to pull in as the surging current propelled them closer and closer to the precipice. Dave and Rick were in the lead and growing increasingly worried as they now could see the spray from the waterfall and knew they must do something fast. And then they saw a small opening ahead between two small cedars only a few feet from the lip of the falls. With frantic strokes they swung their craft into the narrow entrance. Dave leaped out of the bow and landed in shallow water and hauled the canoe forward to dry land as Rick grabbed the tangled myrica bushes lining the edge.

Right behind came their friends hoping to land in the same spot only there wasn't any room. If they did not land now they would go over the falls and probably not survive as it was very high. On their old map it appeared to be a 50 foot straight drop.

Back paddling wildly Chico and John tried desperately to slow their craft down as they turned sideways in the strong current and waited for the others to pull up their canoe far enough so they could enter the small spot. Inch by inch they fought their way closer to safety but the strength of the river held them in its terrifying grip and began to pull the stern towards the edge.

"Come on John." screamed Chico, "Paddle harder! Harder or we're gonners!"

Rick stepped out into the water and grasped a rope on the bow of their canoe and began pulling them closer to shore.

"That was way too close for comfort." Chico breathed with a sigh of relief as he swung a leg out on dry ground.

"Let's go take a look at this thing." drawled John as he stood up and stretched his limbs. His heart was still beating rapidly and his arms felt like lead.

After climbing down through a maze of boulders and around a series of trees the group were soon looking up at three great cascades of frothing water that tumbled over a series of drops ending in a deep green pool at the bottom.

"Let's have lunch and do a little fishing," yelled Dave over the roar of the falls. Without hesitation the men unlashed their fishing rods that had been secured to the gunnels and John had found the earthworms still alive and tucked away in an old tobacco can. In a few minutes the worms were sailing through the air and plopping gracefully in the pool at the foot of the third falls.

Dave felt a nibble on his line, then another as his bait was carried to the back of the pool.

"I got one, " he yelled as he pulled in a foot long trout. Next to him Chico gave him a blank stare as he retrieved his untouched lure. Looking over at John he saw him snap his rod up straight as a brookie struck hard. The fish raced across the pool towards a dark corner and then fled downstream in the fast water. John pumped his rod vigorously as he pulled the pugnacious fish through the water.

"You really know how to catch those big ones John." quipped Dave as he viewed the small thrashing fish on the end of the line. John gazed at the multi-colored circles on the side of the trout as it gleamed in the bright sunlight. He marveled at it's beauty. This was one of the reasons they all loved to spend time in the outdoors, catching the wild and beautiful brook trout.

As they stood silently fascinated with the small fish they heard a snort some distance away.

"I wouldn't even bother wasting my time fishing for those minnows." Rick chortled as he took his rod apart. As he spoke the sound of line being run off on Chico's reel brought him up short. He was fascinated as his friend brought in the largest fish yet.

"I'll watch for awhile and maybe you'll catch enough for lunch," and laughed.

"You go ahead Rick and start a fire and start frying up the fish." Chico responded.

"Good idea, who brought a frying pan?" Rick looked at each of the men.

"Nobody brought one, did they? John you always bring extra stuff, how could you forget?"

"Well, I have an idea fellas." John replied as he began collecting some very small sticks for a fire. Rick watched him but was now crunching down on an apple, as it was doubtful they would have cooked fish for lunch.

Dave had quit fishing and was leaning back against a flat rock resting in the warm sun. He watched John place a flat, very thin slab of rock on top of two upright slabs to make a platform over the small pieces of wood he had collected.

"There we'll try that," he stated and proceeded to light a small piece of birch bark under the small twigs. "Sure wish we had some butter to grease my rock."

Small flames began beating against the bottom of the top slab and smoke began to curl out from under the small canopy.

"It won't be long now and that will be hot enough to cook our fish." he commented.

The others had doubtful looks but Chico had cleaned the fish and now brought over some small fillets. Within a short time the fish were frying on the top rock and Rick was yelling, "Come and get your hors d'oeuvres fellas, cheese and crackers." He proceeded to lay them on a large rock and Chico pulled out a few cans of fruit from his sack. Dave opened his eyes and decided he liked the aroma of frying trout and with some effort he arose from his seat of comfort. "Okay ole buddy I'm ready for some of that fine smelling food." he crackled.

"Come and try some of this." called out John as he lifted a small fillet from the steaming rock. "I think it's cooked through."

Chico had grabbed a piece and began to gingerly nibble on the hot trout.

"Not bad, not bad at all." he commented to the others.

The group soon settled into the fine gourmet of cheese and crackers, fried brook trout and sweet butterscotch pudding all washed down with ice cold water from the Aubinidong River.

"Sunshine, good food and a beautiful wilderness setting, what more could we ask for?" remarked Rick as he stretched out a nearby rock.

"Not much for sure," replied Dave, "Except to make it safely to the vehicles before dark."

"Yes and on that note we'd better be moving along," John stated as he unfolded an old weather beaten map that had seen far better days. "It would appear by this map we have a long way to go."

Rick was already heading for the canoes with his gear. "Let's go, time's a wasting and the days a passing."

Horseflies and huge deer flies buzzed around them looking for a place to land on exposed skin as they headed out unto the water. The two canoes quickly shot through the first set of riffles. Glad to be back on the water the foursome maneuvered around the rocks in the shallow parts of the river. They were constantly looking and listening for changes in the river as the map had indicated they had one more falls to circumvent.

The sun had begun to slip lower in the sky and long dark shadows were forming along sections of the water. There were still a large number of rocks above and below the water they had to watch out for. Rick and Dave's canoe could not take many more hits after the many hard smashes it had taken. Nevertheless they surged ahead which appeared reckless abandon to their two friends who followed with a little more care. John hoped not to destroy his own canoe if at all possible.

Sweeping through set after set of shallow rapids it seemed to Chico that the sight of trees, rocks and water would never end. Lining the canoes through boulder strewn riffles only seemed to increase his feeling of awareness of the oncoming evening and all the perils that lay ahead of them. To be caught on the river at night could end up a nightmare.

John was thinking they had been paddling a long time when they came around a corner of the river and saw Rick and Dave pulling ashore far ahead of them.

"It's the other big falls John," sang out Chico.

His partner felt a little nervous in the stern as he recalled the close call at the last falls. The current had begun to pick up speed and both men hoped to land where the others had. The sound of the roaring cascade came to their ears as they drew closer. A film of vapor rose above the lip of the falls which only increased the men's stress level.

"I wish we could find a landing spot a little further from the falls," John croaked.

"Those two are almost at the brink again." Dave and Rick had pulled their canoe up out of the way and were waiting for their friends to come ashore. They watched with amusement as the big canoe angled its way towards the small opening. The adrenalin rush had begun again for Chico and John as they knew they could not afford to misjudge the speed or direction as they approached. A miscalculation would send them quickly over the edge.

The flat bottom canoe moved slowly closer and seemed to hesitate in the swirling mass of black water beneath them. The heavy brush along the shore was enticingly close as John allowed the craft to swing sideways and then the two paddled with lunging strokes and the canoe shot forward into the opening.

"Good going fellas" sang out Rick as Chico sprang from the bow and pulled the canoe safely up on shore.

And now came the time for hard labor as they began the exhausting job of tugging and pulling the two canoes through the tangled brush and over the multitude of intertwining cedars that hampered their way. Sometime later they finally approached the edge of the river bank near the foot of the great falls. The thundering roar was deafening as the four exhausted men gazed upward at the spectacular display above them.

Richard wiped the sweat and water spray from his dark face and began looking for a place to launch the canoes. Channels of rushing water curled around huge rocks as the river continued to drop for the next quarter mile. There was no possible way to maneuver through the fast current and miss all the obstacles.

"Come on!" he roared and grasping the end of his canoe he headed back into the dense cover of the forest dragging it behind him. The others soon followed. Thrusting their bodies through the closely knit scrub brush the exhausted men fought their way over and around the many deadfalls and stumps that impeded their way. At times lifting the canoes and other times pulling and shoving they moved ahead slowly, occasionally with a muffled grunt or mutter when one would slip or trip on the uneven ground.

As they began to edge closer to the river they all began to take notice that the forest had grown darker and the water in the river had taken on a deeper shade of blue. The sun was dropping in the western sky and time was a major factor if they hoped to be off the river by nightfall. Finally they arrived at the shoreline and began to assess the swifts that lay ahead.

John took one last look at the booming falls and a terrifying thought crossed his mind. To have been propelled over that falls would have been certain disaster. Little did he know that only a short week before two unfortunate canoeists from the States had been swept over with catastrophic results. One man did not survive. Chico and he jumped into their craft and followed their friends downstream as the gray of evening began to descend and the shadows grew darker. Now with only one thought they paddled with their strength fading through the endless rocks that filled the small rapids. No longer as careful as they had been they swept forward oblivious to the scraping and grinding they heard from under the canoe.

Finishing before dark was all they had on their minds. Mile after mile fell away as they paddled furiously hoping to make their bush buggy before nighttime. The long summer evening was drawing to a close and the black water made it difficult to gage the speed of the current or make out the rocks.

John could barely see their companions ahead but could hear the canoe hitting the unseen boulders as they swept through them.

"We'd better go ashore Cheek." he said, "It's getting too dark."

"Okay, but what about those guys?" Chico nodded towards the disappearing canoe far ahead.

"They'll have to get off the river soon or they could have big trouble." John muttered with considerable worry etched on his face. The two men directed their canoe into a small opening and disembarked.

"Man it's dark in here and we won't make it far before we can't see at all." John remarked as the two peered into the snarled mass of black trees that lay ahead.

"Come on friend, let's see how far we can go through this stuff," replied Chico as he lifted the front of the heavy craft. He was looking ahead for a passage through the heavy brush when he turned and yelled back, "Look John, isn't that a clearing on the rise ahead? Putting down the canoe he began pointing at an area that was brighter than the other parts of the bush around them.

"Thank the Lord," came the reply, "You're right Chico, I remember now the map does show some kind of trail along the river about two miles above King's Shoots. King's Shoots was a serious set of small falls and rapids where the group had left the bush buggy that would transport them back to the vehicle at the top of Gong Lake where their adventure had begun.

"You mean we have to carry this monstrosity for two miles in the dark?" growled his partner.

"That's right old pal." he replied with a crooked smile. Even exhausted as he was he was pleased they were done with the river. Somehow they would manage on the trail.

"Well it's great we found the road but we can barely see already." Chico rasped.

John shrugged as he tied in the paddles and slipped his packsack on. Together they hoisted the ninety pound weight up on their shoulders and began pushing their way through the last few yards of dense brush keeping the clearing in sight ahead of them.

They soon found themselves on an overgrown logging road that led both ways. Visibility on the old trail was far better as they began the long carry but the footing was precarious and difficult with the weight on their shoulders. Their feet slipped and sunk in the black oozing muck in the bog holes on parts of the road. With overwhelming exhaustion but determination they plodded forward through the long stringy grass that covered the pathway and hid many of the ruts made in years past. The tight grass continually wrapped around their ankles causing them to trip and lurch out of control sending the canoe flying off their shoulders.

To add to their hardships the mosquitoes and black flies had multiplied by the millions since arriving on shore, flying in their eyes and up their noses. Every so often one of them would start choking or coughing violently after swallowing one of the little critters.

Suddenly Chico stumbled on a large chunk of ground rising unseen under his feet. Skidding sideways he went to his knees and both men collapsed under the canoe.

"Time for a rest," Chico gasped and flipped the heavy canoe off their shoulders.

"I wonder where those two are," rasped John. "It's far too dangerous to be on the water now."

Looking through the trees they could see the river not far away black and ominous and wondered how they could ever find their friends in the dark.

"Listen, do you hear that?" Chico asked as he held up his hand. Both men stood very still on the dark pathway hearing the sounds of the night. From above came the sound of flapping wings and close by the croaking of an old bull frog. The singing of millions of crickets could be heard in the clear night air, first in a high crescendo and then falling to a low tremor. A small rustling noise in the brush nearby indicated some of the small animals of the woods were coming out to forage for food.

"There they are." sang out Chico. From somewhere in front of them came a loud cracking noise followed by a muffled curse. They continued to stare into the darkness when at last two barely discernible forms emerged from the tree line and began to head towards the tote road dragging their canoe over a series of fallen trees that impeded their path.

"You guys alright?" Chico yelled to the two figures once he could see they had made it to the trail.

"Yeah we're fine but where are we?" Dave asked.

"Only a mile and a half to go." came the reply.

"You sure John this road will take us to the buggy?" Rick asked, He never was absolutely sure his friend really knew where they were?"

"Positive, let's go!" John answered.

The stars had begun to appear as the night closed around them. The four dark forms moved slowly and carefully along the tote road occasionally slipping and sliding in the muddy ruts. The night was clear and the moon had risen over a far hill which helped to illuminate their way. The day had been long and warm and the weight of the canoes had drained the men of their remaining energy and they were thankful the road was easier than the overgrown scrub bush they had bashed through on the portages.

A short time later the four worn out men spotted the little bush buggy in a clearing. John's injured knee was aching and was seizing up. He knew he wouldn't be making it to work for 6 a.m. the following morning.

"Let's find a motel at Aubrey Falls. "Rick suggested. They still had to go back and get the other vehicle and it would take hours for them to drive home.

"That sounds like a great idea." Dave replied as he settled into the back seat of the little V.W. bush buggy.

"Maybe we can make it by midnight." Chico quipped as he closed his eyes and listened to the roar of the engine. They soon were barreling down the dirt road thankful for making it back safely.

The end.

Written by John Gearey

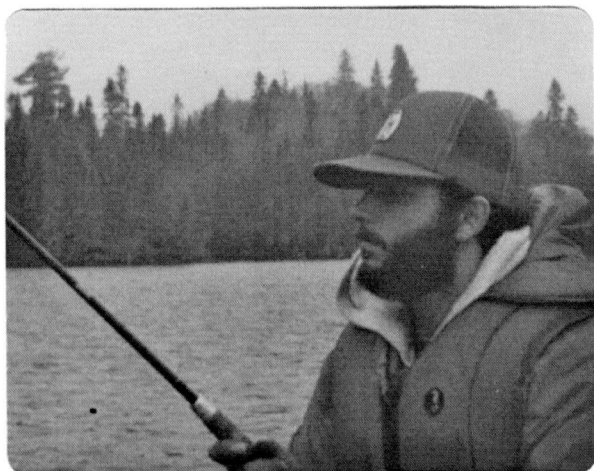

The Author and Chico

A Risky Undertaking

The morning air was crisp and cold as three men stepped out on the frozen surface of Gamitigama Lake in Lake Superior Park. All three walked briskly without snowshoes on the ice as the snow had melted during the warm days of April. They were brimming with confidence and looked forward to a week-end of ice fishing on a small lake in the middle of the Park. Heavy packs were slung on their backs containing all the things needed to survive a couple of days of winter camping.

April had arrived in the north with the days warm enough to melt the snow but the nights cold enough to form a crust on top.

Far to the east the tip of the sun peaked over a hill and spilled a few rays across their path. The sharp early morning air was invigorating as they hiked swiftly along with visions of huge speckled trout dancing in their heads. They marveled at the deep stillness on the lake as the only sound they heard was the crunch of winter boots on the hard packed ice and the deep intake of their breath.

"We'll swing right past the first island" Chico sang out to his brother-in-law Mike a young man of twenty, tall, strong and athletic. He had looked forward to this winter outing that Chico had promised him for some time. Chico had also promised his wife that he would take care of her baby brother as he was inexperienced in camping in the snow.

John the other member of the trio had persuaded them that all would go well and they would return safely and hopefully with lots of fish. He had been on several winter camping trips in the past and the other men felt comfortable in venturing into the interior of the park with him even with the nights still very cold.

"Sure hope the snow in the bush is as easy to walk on as this ice is," chortled Mike as he took a look at the snow covered ground beyond the shoreline. He had worn a pair of old insulated leather work boots that he felt would keep his feet warm enough in light of the warmer days but knew he needed to stay on top of the hard crust formed from the cold night.

"We"ll be fine, as long as we get there before the day warms up." John replied. His only concern was that Mike could freeze his feet in the thin boots. Chico gave his friend a nod as he knew the consequences of traveling on crusted snow once it begins to deteriorate.

In a short time they had made their way past the island on their left and headed south across a large bay. John loved these early morning tramps. He felt healthy and strong and life was good. Once across the bay they filed through a narrows that brought them to a small pond. A barely visible slash on an old birch tree indicated the way to the next lake. The trail led up the side of a steep hill between a stand of hardwoods where the sun barely penetrated and left the area in dark shadows. Chico moved ahead and began to climb the grade with some difficulty.

The crust on the surface was hard and slick. The moisture from a recent rain had permeated the winter snow resulting in a frozen ice surface. He slipped and slid on his side towards the edge of a deep ravine. Grabbing a small tree he scrambled to his feet with his pack still on his back and began pulling himself up one tree at a time to get to the top.

The other two creeped up the slope with care hanging unto the trees around them. Breathing heavily they finally joined their partner.

"Whew, that was a tough climb." rasped Mike as he tried to regain his breath.

Chico was busy rubbing one of his hands. "That's for sure, I cut some of my knuckles on the crust when I fell."

"Yeah and I scraped my knee when I slid into a tree." the oldest member added.

"Aw, quit your bellyaching and let's get going." Mike grumbled. John gave the younger man a look of disdain and headed down the portage trail. They soon worked their way out into a large meadow. By now the sun had risen above the tree tops and was reflecting brightly off the snow. Shielding their eyes from the brilliant rays they could make out the evergreens that edged the meadow, some tamaracks, some balsams and several cedars. A small stream could be seen meandering its way through the crust covered marsh. John headed towards the end following the small creek.

"Be careful fellas, we don't want to slide into the water. It'll be some cold." commented Chico.

"We don't want to lose you just yet Mike." John added.

Mike had made his way up the side of a large snowdrift that hung part way over open water.

"Any fish in there?" he yelled to the other men.

"Naw, its too shallow, but be careful up there." The older man stopped to watch Mike.

They moved forward and followed the curves of the stream keeping at a safe distance, then filed past a tiny frozen pond and through an area of scrub alders that lead to Picea Lake.

"Does it have any fish in it?" Mike asked.

"Don't know." came the reply.

"Why not stop and try it? We can camp right here."

"Maybe some other time." John and Chico had agreed on a plan earlier. They would hike half way down Picea then strike through the forest using a compass to find the lake they planned to camp on.

Picea Lake appeared ahead of them through the sparse trees. The lake was long and narrow and resembled an airport runway having no islands or protruding rocks.

"Sure looks like a great lake to me." Mike wished he hadn't volunteered to carry the ice auger.

A short time later they made it to the mid point of the lake on the east shore.

"Let's take a rest." Chico grunted. He slid his pack off and climbed up on a large cedar tree that lay on the shoreline. Half covered by a snowdrift it had been uprooted by a storm years past and its massive size was a reminder of the days when it stood tall and strong.

John took out a topo map of the area and spread it open on the tree for the others to see.

"We'll leave from here," he said pointing a finger to a spot on the map, "and hike over to this small lake and then we'll head for Paradise Lake."

Chico felt comfortable with the plan. Cutting across country made sense as it was a shorter route and the hiking would be easy and fast on the crusted snow. This was a good time to travel through the woods. Once spring came the undergrowth and fallen trees would make it difficult walking. Later in spring it would be easier to follow the portage trails.

Mike stood silently with his pack still on his back. He was eager to stay on the move and find the lake they planned to fish as soon as possible.

John and Chico helped each other put on their pack sacks. Chico looked over at Mike and smiled at the small size of the sack on his back. His own pack was heavy and carried the three man tent, sleeping bag, food and cooking utensils making it bulky as well.

"Let's move." he bellowed and headed into the heavy brush. The terrain proved to be moderately hilly with hardwoods on the ridges and a mix of conifers in the basins. The three men kept a straight course due east and soon came to a small lake nestled in a shallow valley.

"What a pretty little lake." commented Chico. They paused

on the edge of the forest to look across.

"What is that in the middle?" Mike asked, staring at a large dark spot.

"It's not moving." Chico answered, "Let's go see, fellas."

John was already heading across the ice towards the spot when suddenly he began sinking in the snow along the edge of the lake. The morning sun had begun penetrating the crust, making it soft. By afternoon there would be water on the surface and deep slush.

As they moved across the lake they were able to make out a large beaten down area. Coming closer they could see brown tufts of hair and bones of all sizes scattered about in the snow. Deep dark blotches of blood were spread throughout the entire area.

They stood silently staring at what had been a great tussle of life and death. The surrounding forest seemed to have taken on an aura of deep solemnity that paid homage to the death of a majestic animal. The trees hardly stirred in the light breeze. Each man envisioned in his own mind the death struggle of the valiant moose as it vainly attempted to fight off the hungry wolf pack. The fear and the ferociousness of the wilderness had played itself out in the middle of this small lake.

John felt a touch of sadness as he turned and headed for the bush.

Pulling out his compass he took a glance and then entered the trees. His friends followed murmuring quietly to themselves.

The crust on the surface of the snow was still firm in the shade and carried them easily as they moved on.

In a short time they stood on the western shore of Paradise Lake. The lake surface had turned soft as the sun increased in strength and the men stood soaking in the warm rays letting their bodies relax.

Now they would begin to drill holes in the ice and set up lines. However they knew that as the day progressed the snow and ice would deteriorate making the walking difficult and almost impossible among the trees. They would need to travel the next morning very early to stay up on the crust of the snow. To-morrow promised to be another day much the same as to-day, beautiful but potentially disastrous for walking.

Mike had scurried out a few feet from shore and began drilling two holes. The slush had risen around his feet and he hoped the water would not penetrate his leather boots as wet feet would create a cold and miserable experience.

Quickly Chico unstrapped his pack and located a fishing line and a small tackle box inside and prepared to head down the lake. John meanwhile found a large bare rock jutting out of the snow and climbed up unto it.

"Feel a little tired, chum?" asked Chico as he took a long drink from his canteen.

"Somewhat." he responded. The sun beat on his face and he felt warm and comfortable. He licked his lips as he reached for a drink and some lip balm. This was not a time to get lazy, they had lots to do.

"Where do you think we should set up camp?" he asked.

Chico was looking out over the lake wondering the same thing.

"Perhaps we should fish this lower part now and later head up to the other end."

The lake was formed like an hour glass and the upper end being deeper should hold bigger fish.

John had watched Mike drill his holes and it had taken a considerable time. The task had proved far more difficult than the young man had imagined. For Chico and he, it meant more sweat and sore muscles but they needed to drill their holes now as their bodies were starting to cool down from the long hike.

Looking upwards towards the sun he didn't feel like working or even moving. He was enjoying the granola bar in his hand and chewed off the end as he watched Mike feed a line down the hole in the ice with a hook and gob of worm. He wondered how the big dew worm felt as it entered the icy water.

Meanwhile Chico had taken the ice auger and marched down the shoreline some two hundred feet to a small bay and was drilling a hole.

"Ah well." he thought and jumped down from the rock.

Chico had stood the auger upright on the ice so he went and retrieved it and headed for the opposite side of the small lake.

Three hours passed as the men jigged their lures and basked in the sunlight. The warmth radiated off the white surface of the lake, turning their faces red. They talked and visited and drilled several holes while trying a variety of tackle but only two small trout had been foolish enough to take the bait.

"I thought you said there were lots of fish in this lake?" grumbled Mike to his brother-in-law.

"Alright, let's pull up our lines and head up to the other end of the lake." Chico muttered.

He yelled across to John and pointed in the direction they were to head. His friend immediately began to pull up his lines in order to join them.

A few minutes later they had made their way to a far bay in the upper portion of the small lake.

"Remember the big ones we caught here last May, John?" Chico asked.

"Sure do," his friend replied, "What say we set up our tent here on the ice and fish till dark."

Mike took a look at the two men who were busily unfolding the tent.

"What about supper guys?" he blurted. Hunger pangs had set in and he felt famished.

"Supper!" John looked over at the two men. "Are you making supper Cheek?"

Chico his face already brown from the sun, glanced over. "Only if we're going to have fresh fish over an open fire."

"Well Mike, you'd better start catching fish or we're going to starve." John gurgled and gave the young man a big grin.

"Aw come on fellas, I'm hungry."

"Soon as we get the tent set up and a fire going we'll cook supper." Chico replied.

The sun had edged slowly to the brim of a western hill and

great long shadows began to stretch out over the lake.

"Mike, why don't you scrounge around and find some dry wood for a fire while we finish setting up the tent." Chico barked.

The younger man turned and looked at the deep snow along the shore. He'd rather fish or better still he'd rather be eating and relaxing. He began breaking off small dead branches from the spruce trees that grew close to where he stood. Moving further inland he began to sink to his waist in the soft snow under the trees.

"Great trip," he muttered, "No fish, I'm wet and it's going to be cold tonight." The other men had spread a layer of boughs on the ice to place the tent on.

"Let's find a couple of dead trees for a base for the fire." bellowed John as he began walking down the shoreline. Chico began digging out a large area in the snow just off the ice for the fire. The trio continued to make forays into the bush dragging old dead pine limbs and branches to the site.

The sun had disappeared behind a hill and dusk was descending rapidly as they lit some pieces of birch bark under the dead branches. Carefully Chico blew on the spark and a small flame grew, reaching for the larger wood above. "Get the food ready to cook, guys." he sang out.

An hour later, their stomachs full of beans and burnt cheese sandwiches they drank black tea and watched their tip-ups. A full moon had risen illuminating the lake in a peculiar yellow glow. Arrows of light streamed through the tops of the tall maples that stood dark and lonely along the far shore. Long pencil shadows stretched out over the white expanse forcing the visitors to ponder on the strange sight and causing them to wonder of the marvels of nature.

The men fished for some time and watched the fire throw sparks high in the night air as they listened to the occasional sound of the trees in the forest popping from the frost. The night grew colder as they took turns huddling around the fire and checking their fishing lines.

"I'm going to bed." Mike announced abruptly and headed for the tent. His friends watched him disappear inside. Young people get tired too thought Chico, stomping his feet and peering down the hole in front of him.

"We could fish all night in this moonlight." he commented looking over at his chum.

John was staring at his line deep in thought. He could feel the cold as it began to penetrate his clothes and wondered if the tip of his nose had begun to freeze. "Good idea if the fish were biting."

Pulling his hand out of his mitt he held it over the end of his nose. The warmth helped but fogged his glasses and they frosted over immediately.

"Yeah, that's right, no fish at this end of the lake either," Chico groaned. "I'm turning in."

"Me too." came the muffled reply.

The pair headed for the tent. The fire now barely visible had burned deep into the snow, with only a thin strand of smoke rising from the pit.

John buried himself deep inside his mummy sleeping bag designed for cold nights like these. Chico sat folding his clothes at the end of the tent. Methodically he adjusted his own sleeping bag and then rolled up his jacket and placed it at the end for a pillow. Slipping off his heavy damp socks he stuffed them in his sleeping bag to dry out. He wondered if Mike had done the same. As he slid his legs into the bag he thought he heard a noise outside. John gave a short snort beside him. Both of his friends were asleep. He sat still listening and then he heard the noise again. From far down the lake came a low pitched wail. A few seconds later another longer one, much closer. He felt a chill run down his spine. There was no mistaking the sound. A wolf pack was close. Probably the same pack that had killed the moose on the other lake. Laying back, he zipped up his bag and waited with eyes wide open. Before long his eyelids began closing but he continued to strain his ears for another sound but the night was quiet. Finally he slept.

Later in the night, John woke with a start. He sat up and

looked at the others sleeping peacefully. He wondered what had brought him out of his deep sleep. Likely too much black tea. He knew he had to go out. He resisted the thought. It was going to be cold out there, very cold.

A booming sound split the night air. He sat upright, his heart beating rapidly. The sound came again and was closer. Climbing out of his sleeping bag he unzipped the front door and peered out into the night. All seemed well. He put on his jacket and reached for his boots stiff from frost. Finally he stepped out on the ice and looked around. The cold night air slowly pierced his cotton long johns. He could feel cold icy fingers wrap themselves around his bony legs. The need to relieve himself became overwhelming as he fumbled with his drawers.

Looking skyward he saw wave after wave of fluctuating light pass across the night skies. The man stood transfixed wishing his friends could see the display of colors as the aurora borealis lit up the heavens. What majesty! He gave God thanks for these wonderful sights.

"Craaaaack, crack," John stood very still. A loud cracking, booming sound was moving across the lake towards him. He remained beside a fishing hole they had filled with some snow to keep it from freezing. As he watched he could make out a large crack coming quickly across the surface of the ice while the noise grew louder. Suddenly the hole beside him sent a puff of water high in the air, and the crack continued to move on in a crooked path. John was amazed at how the ice would expand and move in such a way and then he quickly headed for the tent and the warmth of his down sleeping bag.

Mike opened his eyes. Morning had arrived. Frost hung heavy on the interior of the tent made from the moisture of their breath. He felt chilled and didn't want to move. Maybe somebody would get the fire going and start breakfast. He looked over at his brother-in-law who was awake and looking at him.

"What are you guys doing, still laying here?" he rasped.

"The sooner you get up and get the fire going the better." Chico replied with a grin.

The day was young and the air was cold as Mike crawled from his sleeping bag. He had slept with all his clothes on. John woke up and reached for his pants wishing he had kept them in the bag with him. They had frozen stiff over night from the knees down.

The three campers stepped out into the frosty morning. Finding wood was difficult but the men driven by need searched the shoreline for dry twigs and dead branches.

In a short space of time they had a can of water hanging above a small fire. Mike began drilling another fishing hole as the other two tried to find some warmth from the tiny flame.

"We'll have to head back early fellas. Once the sun hits the snow it melts fast." Chico remarked. "We'll be lucky if the crust holds us at all, if its as warm to-day as yesterday."

"Let's leave within the hour, fish or no fish." John took a swallow from his steaming cup of coffee and watched Mike clean out the ice covered holes.

The sun had begun to rise over the top of the hill to the east as the two older men rolled up their sleeping bags and took down the tent. They quietly went about their tasks feeling a little down because the fish were not biting. They had discussed earlier how good this lake had been the previous spring but now seemed to be dead.

Their packs were soon loaded and only the lines were left to retrieve and pack away.

"Come on Mike and get packed up, it's 8 o'clock and time to leave." Chico yelled.

"Hang on Cheek." Mike responded. He watched one of the long slender gads that held his fishing line begin to twitch. Suddenly it gave a hard jerk and the end of the willow stick disappeared down the hole.

"Fish on!" he screamed and dove across the ice to grab the line. Giving a hard upward pull to set the hook he began to bring the fish up hand over hand. He had discarded his mitts but the cold seemed to have little effect on his hands as he worked the line feverishly. This was the first fish of the trip and he was excited.

The struggling trout came up through the hole flapping in the air with the brilliant colored spots on its sides glistening in the sun.

"What a fish!" roared John as he came running over to see the splendid specimen. "Congratulations!"

"Look at that beauty!" Mike proudly held the fish high and turned to show the other men.

However Chico was not paying attention, he was bent over another hole bringing in a fish.

"The fish are finally biting." he gurgled with delight as a large trout landed on the ice beside him.

Meanwhile John had headed for a nearby hole where a gad had been pulled far down and was jerking sporadically. Landing on his knees he grasped the line and felt the fish move so he gave it some slack letting it run as it felt heavy. Then with a jerk he set the hook and brought it up to the aperture coaxing it carefully away from the jagged edges of the ice that could cut the line. With one last pull the trout came out and landed near him. For a moment he stood staring at the beautiful fish laying at his feet. At this moment the fish represented all that was wild and beautiful, nature personified and now it lay before him dying.

Picking it up he marveled at it's beauty and the multi ringed spots of different colors glistening in the sun. What a shame to keep something like this and for a short moment considered releasing it back down the hole. After a pause he slid the fish into a plastic bag. That was a lot of fish and would make a tasty meal.

The action continued as strike after strike came. More fish were caught, most of them large for brook trout and many more were lost and the bait stolen. Excitement was in the air and time sped by with the three men running from one hole to the next. The sun stood high in the sky before the biting abated and they all felt warm and happy with how the morning had gone.

"We'd better be going lads, it's a long walk out." John sang out. He knew they had already stayed far too long and the walking would be very difficult at this time of the day.

"Let's stay for another half hour. The fish are still biting." Mike retorted, he had waited a long time to catch some fish.

"Alright," Chico answered. He was happy that his brother-in-law had finally caught some fish and was having fun.

The strikes came much slower as time progressed but the men seemed reticent to leave this small corner of the wilderness.

Another hour passed before John looked at his watch and then without a word he pulled up his lines and stuffed them in his sack. Mike was standing by a hole hoping to catch one more fish to make his limit.

"I'm going fellas," John sang out as he slung his pack on his back. "The crust will be soft already."

"I'm toasting a sandwich first." Mike stated as headed for the fire.

"We'll catch up soon." Chico nodded at his friend who was already on the move heading for the far shore.

As he moved across the surface of the lake he began sinking deep in the slush nearly to the top of his insulated rubber boots. Once in the soft snow drifts on the edge of the lake he sank to his hips with every step. He pushed on until he reached the shady area under the trees. The exertion had made him sweat, he would need to peel off his sweater and drink lots of fluid. Testing the strength of the snow he found the crust still held in the areas the sun had not penetrated, however around bigger trees the walking was tricky as some snow was still firm while other spots were weak.

Taking out his compass he took a reading that would bring him to the small lake where the moose had died. The going was slow and arduous as he often sunk a foot or more in the deteriorating snow. As he suspected when he stayed in the shadows he didn't sink as much and at times was able to stay on top. However close to the big hardwoods he sank quickly to his hips. He knew this would be a long walk in the warm spring sun as he was overheated already. Taking another long drink from his canteen he turned and looked back. There was no sign of the others so he moved on.

Some time later Chico and Mike followed John's water filled tracks across the lake. The sun was high in the sky, and a soft warm breeze fanned their sunburned faces. Water sloshed over their boots as they reached the shore and they knew they should have left hours earlier. This was turning out to be an ordeal.

Chico moved ahead and followed the footsteps of the man who had gone ahead but sunk deep in the snow with every step. In a few moments they found their pants soaked from the moisture in the melting snow.

"We'll have to stay away from John's trail." he called back to his brother-in-law who had fallen back a short distance but could hear him complaining.

"Awww!". Mike let out a roar. Chico looked back and saw him submerged to his waist in a drift.

"Are you okay?" he hollered.

"Sure, I'll be alright, I think I skinned my shin on a log under the snow." Mike replied in a crackling voice.

Chico watched from a distance as the younger man tried to extricate himself from the three foot crevice he was entangled in. He shook his head as his friend rolled out on his side on the third attempt. Mike was using up a lot energy each time he sank and was getting frustrated. Moving quickly ahead he would glimpse back occasionally and could tell Mike was falling further behind as he struggled with the conditions.

Sweat beads formed on Chico's forehead as he rounded a small knoll covered with maple trees. Some fifty feet ahead stood John leaning on a large yellow birch tree watching him.

"Where"s Mike?" he asked as his chum drew closer.

"He's having a little trouble in the snow." came the reply. "Wish we'd started back sooner."

"That's for sure," John snorted looking back in the bush for their companion. "My legs are soaked."

Chico proceeded to take off his pack and peel off his light jacket. The fish were adding to the weight and he could feel his shoulders tiring.

"Let's go, I'm cooling down." John said and turned to go.

"You go ahead, I'll wait for Mike to catch up." Chico sat down on an ancient stump wondering where the young man might be.

"Okay. I'll wait for you over on Picea." came the reply.

Chico watched him disappear through the myriad of grey trees. He could see no sign of Mike which worried him as it had been a long time since he last saw him. Closing his eyes he rested, and listened to the sounds of small birds and the faint groanings of the tree limbs as they moved in the light breeze. He opened his eyes a few minutes later and peering through the deep shadows he could dimly make out a dark outline of an approaching figure. Breathing a sigh of relief he jumped to his feet.

"Mike, how are you doing."

"Terrible, how come we didn't bring snowshoes?"

Chico could see the frustration in his eyes.

"Yes it would have been better."

"I can't take a step without falling through." Mike complained. "My legs are banged up, they're wet, and my boots are soaked through."

"Well let's keep going or we'll get hypothermia." croaked Chico.

"I'm too tired to keep going." Mike spouted, throwing his small sack near the stump and sitting down.

"Okay. Mike but I've cooled off and need to keep moving. I'll see you over on Picea Lake and don't wait too long."

Chico picked up his pack and tromped off. Behind him he thought he heard the young man mumble, "Maybe you will and maybe you won't."

❧

John meanwhile had continued forward stepping gingerly on the weakened crust. Every few steps he plunged deep in the decaying snow. By early afternoon he had crossed the small lake and moved on to the eastern shore line of Picea Lake. Finding a large fallen tree he scrambled up on it and dug around in his sack till he found a hunk of cheese and a roll of salami. The sun was intense for this time of the year and he decided to relax for a while and eat his food and drink some of the stale water left in his canteen. Looking back through the trees he could see no sign of his partners. They sure were taking their time. As the time passed he grew restless waiting and finally decided to hike to the far end of the lake and wait for them there.

Chico had walked but a short distance after leaving Mike when he decided he'd better stop and wait for him again. The tall young man was moving towards him slowly. The snow was collapsing underneath him and he was sinking deep into the underbrush. As he drew closer Chico could see fatigue etched on his long drawn face mixed with frustration.

"I can't believe we're doing this." Mike lamented bitterly.

"Hang in there bud, you'll make it. Keep moving and don't get too upset." Chico replied, and began walking, but was pleased that the young man was at least still willing to move.

Behind him he heard a curse. Turning he watched Mike plunge face forward into a hump of snow and sink slowly down. He lay motionless for a few moments, then rolled over and sat up. Chico could see the redness in his face and could hear him cursing.

"Get up and keep moving!" thundered Chico.

"I ain't moving another step." grumbled Mike, pulling his wet, cold legs to his chest. "And where's that so called friend of yours? Nice of him to wait for us."

"He's on the next lake waiting for us, so get up or you're going to freeze right there." Chico's voice was edged with disgust.

Mike did not move. Chico started to move towards him and changed his mind and turned and headed through the trees following John's tracks.

"Go ahead and leave, I told you I ain't moving." Mike's voice echoed through the bush.

His brother-in-law kept going forward hoping the young man would not give up and just lay in the snow. Being covered in sweat and exhausted Mike could succumb to hypothermia relatively quickly.

John was sunning himself at the north end of Picea Lake when he saw a lone figure coming down the lake towards him. Chico was coming quickly spraying slush and water in his wake and could see his chum was somewhat irritated even from a distance.

"Where's Mike?" John asked as his friend came closer. Chico threw off his pack and reached in and found some beef jerky. Sweat streamed down his dark red face as he sank down on the pack.

"I'm not sure," he responded, "I left him a few hundred yards east of Picea. He said he was not going any further. Said he's finished. I guess he wore himself out from falling through the crust and getting angry.

"What do you think we should do?" Chico was deeply worried about the young man and felt a little guilty for leaving him.

John stood up and stretched. He felt like he'd been waiting for hours.

"I'll go back and get him."

"He said he wouldn't go any further, John. How do you plan to get him moving?" his friend asked.

"Oh, I'm sure he'll come. No one wants to die in the bush no matter how tired they feel." He fished out a pair of dry socks from his pack and headed down the lake.

As he approached the mid point of Picea Lake he could make out someone perched on top of a downed cedar. Mike had pulled himself high above the snow and had both his boots off.

"Are you okay?" John asked, watching him rub his red feet. His companion nodded his head without looking up and kept on rubbing.

"Here's a dry pair of socks, Mike. Put them on and let's go." He lay them on the tree.

"I'll come along, soon." Mike responded.

John watched Mike put the dry socks on over his wet cold feet. Man he thought, he must have endured some real agony with those cold feet. He stooped and picked up Mike's pack as the young fisherman began trying to put his feet back into the wet leather boots.

"Follow me when you're ready big guy." croaked John and strode off down the lake.

Chico had been resting on his pack and watching down the lake for some time when he saw John coming towards him wiping the sweat from his forehead with a large handkerchief.

"How did you do that?" he asked pointing a finger down the lake. John turned and watched Mike trudging towards them with his head down.

"Not much," he replied with a big grin. "Threw him the socks, took his pack and his pride did the rest."

"How you feeling, Mike?" Chico asked as the young man arrived.

"I'm fine. Give me my sack."

John handed it to him and the three headed up the portage trail leading to Gamitigami Lake. Chico took the lead as they walked in silence often sinking deep in the snow. They fought their way across the large meadow the stream ran through. Weariness began to show on their faces. Both the older men had begun to feel the effects of the days struggles and were slowing down. Mike had stayed close behind and spoke very little. Each one looked forward to the end of the journey.

Finally arriving on the last hill overlooking Gamitigami Lake John and Chico stopped to look out over the white expanse that lay before them. Without a word Mike moved past them and hurried down to the lake.

"Wow, look at Mike go." Chico murmured, and shrugged his shoulders. The two friends worked their way forward to the shoreline. The surface was smooth and hard and had held up far better than the smaller lakes. Mike had moved far ahead of them with a swinging step.

"Isn't that amazing. Look at him go." Chico was shaking his head.

"He can visualize the finish line and he's proving he's got more left than we do." John replied with a big grin on his face.

The two men laughed and strode after the disappearing figure.

The End.

Written by John Gearey.

Hoping for an Answer

One morning while sitting with my friend D.J. on the porch of his cabin having a cup of coffee he related to me a most unusual story. The time of the event was before the advent of all terrain vehicles. The time when men walked the rough trails of the forest and could soak in the sounds of nature without the noise now so often heard. I will endeavor to re-tell the story as best I can.

The time of year was late November on a raw overcast day that threatened snow in the Porcupine Mountains of Upper Michigan. The north wind cut sharply against D.J.'s face as he and three friends began a six mile trek to their hunting camp.

The narrow tote road they were on had been used many years ago to haul great white pines to the nearest mill. Trudging along the snow covered road he could envision the teams of horses straining to pull sleds loaded with massive logs. For a moment he thought he heard the creaking of leather and the snorting of the big animals as they blew out volumes of hot air through their extended nostrils.

He stumbled and came awake from his trance to see only his three companions ahead with their bulging packs slung low on their backs and their rifles dangling haphazardly from their shoulders.

From the start of the hike they had been following the footprints of another group larger in number, probably six hunters who were heading the same direction. A single narrow wheel track ran jauntily down the centre of the road.

"What in the world do you think made that wheel mark men?" asked Joe. Although a veteran of bush travel he could not imagine what kind of device was attached to the wheel.

"I don't think it's a wheel barrow." responded D.J. "The wheel mark is too narrow and can you imagine pushing an apparatus with a small wheel through these bog holes or up these steep hills in this slippery soft snow?"

The men could only guess how much sweat and energy was being used to pull or push the device in these conditions.

The day was gray and foreboding with a heavy cloud cover that threatened more snow. The group continued on the old tote road for some time taking only a short break from time to time. They slipped and slid on the hills and tried not to fall into any of the holes or crevices now hidden by a covering of white snow. Their legs and backs began to feel the wear and tear of the difficult terrain as they began to tire.

Rounding a bend in the road they came to a stop and stared at a very unusual sight. On the side of the road sitting majestically on top of a large fallen tree were a dozen bottles of liquor of all shapes and sizes. They stood proudly in a straight line resembling an honor guard waiting for the arrival of someone important.

The hunters moved forward to take a closer look at this remarkable spectacle so far from civilization.

"Have you ever seen anything quite like that before fellas?" asked Bill, a man who had spent many years hunting in the area. Tall, strong and beginning to gray prematurely he resembled the prototype of the wise and experienced outdoors man whom many looked to for sage advice.

"Never in all my life, Bill." replied Joe as he set his pack down and was looking for a log to sit on. A little overweight he was beginning to wear down and needed to rest.

"Look at the sign they left." Bill gave out a great belly laugh and pointed to a long strip of white paper that ran along under the bottles of spirits.

Written in bold dark ink were the words, "WELCOME TO THE CHICAGO BAR, MAKE YOURSELVES AT HOME"

"Don't mind if I do." Joe sang out as he lifted two of the larger bottles from the log.

"To-morrow's your birthday, D.J. and we'll celebrate it for you. We'll have a real good time for sure." With a big grin he tucked the bottles away in his pack.

"They sure must be having a hard time of it to leave their booze behind". D.J. remarked with a twinkle in his eye. "Most guys would die before abandoning their precious alcohol."

"No doubt they packed far too much stuff and never thought they'd find themselves in these kind of conditions." Bill ventured.

The fourth member of their group of four was a pensive and quite man seldom given to opinionated outbursts. His long face and deep set eyes were focused on the scene as he pondered why anyone would carry so many bottles of alcohol so far in the bush.

"Well boys we'd better keep on the move if we plan to make camp by nightfall." he said and picked up his sack and headed down the trail. He knew from past years the hike was long and tiring in the best of weather. Today the old road was covered with six inches of snow that blanketed the ground obscuring many of the ruts and mud holes. Given these conditions they would be late getting to the cabin and totally exhausted.

They soon resumed their trip down the logging road tramping slowly through the snow, occasionally slipping on the ruts or sliding into the watery depressions.

D.J. who was called Don by many wondered how the group ahead was handling the one wheel contraption loaded with the all the gear.

Big Joe was in the lead when he came to an abrupt halt on the lip of a steep hill.

They had traveled less than a mile from the famous Chicago Bar but now the group stared ahead at an assortment of boxes and bags left unceremoniously on the side of the trail. Moving forward they made their way to the stack of supplies and began to look over the different items left behind. A touch of sadness began to pervade the men as their minds tried to understand the dilemma the group from Chicago had found themselves in.

"Imagine that, those poor fellows are even beginning to leave their food behind." Bill stated as he curiously lifted a flap on one of the larger boxes. Inside were boxes of corn flakes, crackers and glass jars filled with an assortment of condiments.

"They sure had a big load." commented Slim.

The men took only a few minutes to inspect the contents of some of the boxes and knew they were unable to carry anything for the other group. Mid day had arrived and the few flakes of snow in the air told them to keep moving.

They had been hiking for a half hour or more when they came around a sharp corner of the road and there before them sat the one wheel contraption they had been following all day. A three quarter bed frame with a twenty inch bicycle wheel in the centre attached by iron rods made up the makeshift device. Along the sides were handles for carrying and a metal tongue extended in the front with a rope attached to it.

The hauling and pushing of the carrier had finally worn the men down.

After abandoning much of their gear they had finally found it too much work and decided to leave it behind.

"The idea had been good to haul stuff on but it would work far better on a smooth surface and not this terrain." Joe commented after inspecting it closely.

"You have to give those guys credit for hauling that thing all this way. So much work and they still had to leave a lot of their supplies behind. I guess they only have their packs now." murmured Bill. "And whatever they can carry in their hands."

"Let's go fellas, the afternoon is moving on and darkness comes early this time of the year." replied Joe as he headed down the trail.

The snow on the road and the conditions began to take a toll on their strength. For several hours they had been tramping with the loads on their back. The weight was pulling on their shoulders and their legs were weakening as they climbed hill after hill.

The wet snow and water on the road had penetrated the leather boots of both Slim and Bill. They now were walking with wet and sore feet and there was still a long distance to hike before they reached the cabin. The group had slowed but they could ill afford to be caught out here after dark and dusk was only a short two hours away.

Sweating and panting they came over a small rise in the road to come face to face with the other group of hunters. Some of the men were sitting on packsacks, while others were stretched out on canvas tarps and all appeared bedraggled and exhausted. The faces of the thinner men seemed worn and drawn while the heavier men had red blotchy cheeks and white foreheads indicating they were drawing on their last reservoir of strength.

On second glance D.J. and his friends could see the group were wearing some of the best quality clothing available but their jackets hung limply and their pants were wet and wrinkled and covered with mud.

"Greetings gentlemen!" Joe yelled ahead to the waiting men. The tired eyes of the gang from Chicago watched the four men approach.

"Howdy," came the languid reply."

"We ran across some of your stuff back aways." D.J. said almost apologetically.

"Yes. We brought too much. We've never been here before and didn't realize the road was that bad." one of the men commented. He was older than the rest and seemed to be more open to sharing their hardships with the new arrivals.

"Are you fellas from the Chicago area?" Joe asked with a big smile.

"Yeah, we should have packed lighter but thought we'd be here for awhile and felt we needed all the stuff." another man answered sullenly.

"D.J. had seen a little humor in the appearance of the six wretched looking men when they first came up to them. However the longer he took in their condition the greater the feeling of sympathy he felt. He wondered how they might give them a hand. They were all stretched to the limit and the look on their faces told of their need of rest.

One of the men sitting on a large pack asked the question they all wanted to know.

"How far is it to the cabins?"

"Oh I suppose about two miles at least." Bill answered.

"Two miles!" exclaimed a big red faced man who was laying partially on the snow behind the others. "I'm not sure I can go another two feet."

D.J. could tell the six men had been in the process of making some kind of a decision when they had come up to them. Now they appeared to be in a turmoil and indecisive of what to do.

"Do you think we can make it by nightfall if we keep going?" the voice came from a small man seated on a new and very wet duffel bag.

"Sure you can," Joe replied, his smiling robust face showed his eagerness to help. "We'll give you a hand, just grab some stuff and we'll take some and that way we'll all make it by dark."

"No thanks," said a man who had come forward and seemed to want to make a decision for the rest. "We were about to set up camp right here. Most of us are too tired to go any further."

D.J. noted that not all of the group from Chicago felt comfortable with his statement, but none seemed ready to object.

"Are you sure you'll be okay tonight, it's going to be cold and it may snow?"

"Sure we'll manage." the man replied and began to open one of the packs. "See you in the morning."

"Well then in that case we'd better be moving on." Joe looked concerned but gave the others a wave and headed down the road.

Snow was coming down heavier as they hurried along with the thoughts of how spending a night in the cold and snow would affect the tired hunters. Bill walked up beside Joe and spoke quietly "Sure going to be a cold night for those city folks to camp out in."

"Yes, the temperature is already dropping and it's hard to tell how good their sleeping bags are."

The four men continued on in silence as the afternoon came to a close. By the time they arrived at the cabin darkness had begun to settle over the area. Only a faint amount of light remained in the west as the men hurried to bring in firewood and kindling.

Their energy was nearly gone but knew the chores had to be

done. They filled the old pot bellied stove with scraps of paper and kindling and soon had it started. Two of the men went to the nearby stream and brought back fresh water.

With the hard exertion from the trek in they all had sweat profusely even though the day had been cold and snowy. Now their body heat was dropping as they cooled down and they all felt chilled and damp. Warmth and good food was needed as soon as possible. Some of the men brought in the packs and put away the gear while Joe pumped up an old well used Coleman stove.

Presently he had thrown steaks and potatoes in a frying pan and put the water on to boil. The inside of the old cabin was cold from being closed up for many long months and would take some time to warm up. The men kept their jackets on while they went about doing odd chores and preparing their beds.

D.J. had opened the door to the stove and taking a look at the few pieces of wood laying on the hearth decided to bring in more logs. "I'm going out to the wood shed guys and get some firewood. I don't think we have nearly enough." He hoped to get the old stove rocking and get the moisture out the camp.

"Yeah, hang on D.J. I'll bring the lantern." Slim replied and put on his gloves. "Give me a minute and I'll light it."

D.J. stepped out unto the porch and stood quietly looking towards the weather beaten shed that held the firewood. Stillness had descended upon the forest with the arrival of darkness. Taking a deep breath he felt at peace now that they had made it to the cabin. Snow was lightly falling but he could see a short distance past the trees surrounding the cabin. How majestic and peaceful winter could be as it replaced the autumn days. His body had begun to relax from the long walk in and his thoughts went back to the gang from Chicago and he wondered how they were faring.

Slim came up behind him holding the glowing lantern. "Hope this snow stops soon, or the deer won't want to travel to-morrow." he murmured and stepped down on the ground.

D.J. remained on the porch and held up his hand for Slim to be silent. He thought he heard a sound. Both men listened intently.

The night was growing colder and very little wind touched their faces. A strange noise came from far off in the woods.

Slim looked back at D.J. and shrugged his shoulders. He had never heard anything quite like it. "What do you figure it is?" he whispered almost reverently.

"Is it possible?" D.J. appeared to be speaking to himself in deep thought. The sound was coming from the direction of the road they had come in on.

"What? What's possible?" Slim broke in.

"Do you think it's possible somebody's coming down the road?"

Then faintly through the night air, so softly the men could hardly hear it, an almost inhuman sound both sickly and deathly.

"Help, help." Someone out in the snowy, cold night was crying out in despair. The two friends looked at each other in wonder. Had they both heard the desperate cry of someone back down the road, or was it the sound of something the surrounding forest was enticing them with.

"Do you think it's one of the Chicago Six?" asked Slim.

"Perhaps," D.J. replied, "but we should walk back down the road and see if anyone is coming. They might need help if what we heard is one of them."

From far down the road another indistinguishable sound came floating through the air, in some ways strangely alarming. The men hastened towards the old tote road hurrying as much as they could in the wet snow.

Slim had blown out the lantern and left it on the porch and now they could see only a few feet ahead of them. They heard no more sounds as they trudged forward, peering down the path in the hope of seeing someone. The two slipped and slid in the darkness but had gone only a few hundred yards when coming around a sharp bend they could see a dark object laying in the centre of the road. Approaching slowly they began to make out the form of a man crawling on his hands and knees with his nose close to the ground. He stopped and raised his head, crying out weakly, "Help, help me, please."

D.J. and Slim stopped and stared, close to disbelief. Obviously the man was in great distress and had to be from the group of men from Chicago. As they moved closer the man looked up and his body sagged as he made out the two men standing above him. Exhaustion and relief etched across the man's face and he collapsed and lay in the wet snow.

Slim knelt beside the man and touched his face. "We're here bud, and we'll help get you to the camp." The man sat up and then as if coming out of dream he stood up and in a frenzy of passion grabbed Slim and gave him a bear hug. In uncontrolled babbling he explained how he had decided to not spend the night in the cold and snow and try and make it to the cabin instead.

Contrary to the advise of his comrades he had struck out on his own. They had begun to set up two tents but they would be cramped inside and he only had a light weight sleeping bag as well. Even though darkness had begun to descend he believed he could follow the old trail to the camp. However in a short time he found himself enveloped in darkness and found it difficult to distinguish between the bush and the tote road. The snow was getting deeper and harder to walk through and he continually slipped, often falling on his side or on his knees. Frustration and weariness caused him to slow to a trudge as he tried to make out the tree line and follow the snow packed trail.

Time passed and the night grew dark, so dark he could hardly see anything in front of him. He had begun to stagger from exhaustion and had failed to rise the last time he fell and it was in this state the two men found him on the ground trying to follow the barely visible snow covered footprints.

D.J. took the thoroughly fatigued man by the arm. "We are only few hundred yards from your cabin and we can help you make it the rest of the way."

The man whose name was Roy seemed to have regained some strength and was able to stumble along behind his new friends mumbling his thanks from time to time.

After some difficult walking they eventually arrived at the cabin of the Michigan group and took him inside. The living area had warmed up and the heat immediately affected the tired man to the point that he collapsed on the sofa near the stove without a word.

Joe always ready to give a helping hand prepared a large bowl of soup and a ham sandwich and woke Roy from his stupor so he could have some nourishment. The others had pulled out his sleeping bag and put it in a far corner with a piece of foam so he stay with them during the night.

Very early the following morning Slim woke up and looked over where Roy had been sleeping but the man was gone. Looking around the big room there was no sign of his pack or clothes. "It appears as if Roy recovered and decided to go over to his cabin." he said as D.J. crawled out of his sleeping bag. The room temperature had dropped dramatically through the night and all the men hurried to get dressed and stoke the fire in order to warm up.

By mid morning the remainder of the Chicago hunters were spotted coming down the road. As they came closer they looked in even worse shape than the day before. The night's sleep had not been of much help. Slim, D.J., Joe and Bill stood on the front porch and waved to the group as they walked to their own cabin some three hundred yards away. Smoke was rising from the chimney and it was evident Roy had gone over to start the fire for his friends and prepare some grub for them.

"Sure was good of Roy to get up early and warm things up for his guys." Bill commented. "I wonder what time he left to go over to the other cabin?"

"One good thing is the guys all survived but it sure would've been cold." someone replied. They all headed back inside where it was warm.

In the early afternoon Joe answered a knock on the front door. Roy the man they had helped the night before and another man said hi.

"Come on in fellows." boomed Joe.

The two entered carrying a large freshly baked cake with a bunch of unlit candles on top. "Happy Birthday D.J.," sang out Roy with a huge grin on his face. "I remember enough from last night that someone said it was your birthday to-day so I just wanted to thank you for saving my skin and thought I'd bake you a cake."

"Thanks Roy and I'll put on fresh coffee and we'll try a piece right now." D.J. hustled about to get forks and cups from the cupboard.

The other man with Roy introduced himself as Bob and he began to tell them how the night before had affected them. "That was the coldest night I've ever experienced in my life, and as soon as I get back to Chicago I'm going to write Ted Williams and give him a piece of my mind!" His face was contorted in an expression of indignation.

"Why? What did Ted Williams a ball player have to do with you spending a night in the cold?" asked Joe in wonderment.

"Cause, just before leaving on this trip I went out and bought a brand new sleeping bag with his name on it, and I nearly froze in it. So I'm going to let him know how I feel."

To this day D.J. still remembers the look on the men's faces as they listened. The sleeping bag Bob had bought was thin and would have been clearly marked for indoor summer time use only. Only made for warm nights they all wonder how he made it through the very cold night while being so totally exhausted.

We close this story with but a small reminder that by the grace of God we make it through each day but it is our responsibility to use the resources he gives us wisely.

The End

Written by John Gearey
April, 2012

Storm over Achigan

The End of the Road

The old beat up Dodge truck with far too many rust spots rumbled down the narrow logging road that led to a lake at the end of the road. Rain was pounding on the two canoes strapped precariously on top and the headlights dimly lit up the innumerable water filled potholes that appeared ahead.

Four individuals rode inside the magnificent three quarter ton truck with off road suspension that could jolt the strongest of vertebrae. Earlier in the week they had decided to spend a weekend camping and fishing in the wilderness and so here they were. Unfortunately the rain had come down all day but had not deterred Rob and Linda as they pulled into their new friends driveway late in the afternoon with great anticipation and ready to challenge the great outdoors. Their packs were stuffed with food, cooking utensils, tent, sleeping bags, rain gear and fishing equipment.

"Are you sure you still want to go?" John asked with a raised eyebrow. The rain was coming down harder and night was fast approaching.

"Sure, we're all packed and ready to go, how about you guys?" Rob responded.

John sensed his friends excitement and how much they looked forward to the trip ahead regardless of the weather.

"Alright, let's get going." he responded and turned to look at his wife Mary. She did not look pleased. The prospect of spending a night camping in the wet bush did not appeal to her.

And now here she found herself peering out the window of a

bucking piece of scrap metal on a water sogged, mud filled road with the rain pouring down. With her neck snapping and her teeth rattling she only knew they were heading for some unknown lake in the middle of nowhere. She wondered why she had ever agreed to come on this crazy outing.

Some serious doubts had begun to form in the minds of the others as well.

"How much further?" groaned Rob as he bounced against the back door of the truck for what felt like the hundredth time.

"At least another five miles." John replied over his shoulder being careful not to lose control of the bucking truck.

"What time is it?" asked Linda who at first had felt thrilled to be heading out but was beginning to question this whole venture. Questions had begun to arise in her mind. What if the old truck broke down so far from civilization? How could they possibly set up the tents in this rain and in the dark?

"It's ten o'clock and dark already?" Mary answered as she shone the flashlight on her watch.

"We'll be at the lake shortly, folks," John added, hoping to give them a lift.

They watched the wipers whip back and forth on the windshield in a futile attempt to keep the rain off. Tree branches scraped the sides of the truck making loud ripping noises as the road narrowed perceptively and had become extremely difficult to see. He slowed the truck to a crawl. The limbs full of wet leaves continually smacked against the windshield often blinding him.

Little more was said as the miles slipped away and then John slowed the truck and came to a stop. He stared into the darkness and could barely make out a rise in the road where a large grey boulder loomed several yards ahead.

The slab of rock appeared as smooth as glass and appeared very steep. Edging the truck forward the group were able to get a better view.

"What's that?" yelped Mary as she strained to make out the obstacle that lay before them.

"It's a small boulder we have to climb over." John responded.

Rob and Linda leaned forward over the front seat and stared. This was no small boulder. To them it appeared very high and very steep.

"We have to drive over that?" Linda asked with a quiver in her voice.

"Oh sure, it won't be a problem." he answered, "Although it will be a little slippery with all the rain."

"What happens if the truck stalls or slips sideways over the edge?" questioned Rob as he recalled reading of stories of four wheel drive trucks rolling over on some of the wild backwood roads.

"I'd rather not think about it." the man murmured as he kept his foot on the brake. "We have to go over it because there is still a half a mile to the lake."

"I'm getting out right here!" Mary stated and opened her door. "I'll walk up, it's a lot safer."

"Yeah, we will too," Rob said softly as he and his wife slid out the back door.

"You're all going to get wet." rasped John

No one took time to answer as all three were busy pulling on their rain suits. John jumped out of the truck and locked in the hubs on the front wheels and then with one last look at the slippery hill he climbed in and began to accelerate the vehicle. Slowly he edged forward and the front end began to rise. He could feel the big knobby tires begin to slip on the wet rock. The tires were good in snow but now here on this smooth polished boulder he had some doubts. Shoving the gas pedal down the front end began to rise and the road disappeared and all that was visible was the hood of the truck. The two dim headlights shone far up in the sky as the old truck climbed higher and higher. He could smell burning rubber and hear the wheels screaming as they tried frantically to grip the rock.

"Come on old fella." he whispered under his breath. For a brief second he felt as if the truck was going over backwards and then the front end came down and leveled off and the thrill of the moment passed.

"That was an eerie feeling doing this at night." he mused. He sat in the truck and recalled how a month ago he had cleared the road of fallen trees and how hard it was to get through the mud holes but in the end it was all worth it as the fishing had been amazing. The lake for some reason had been forgotten for years as there were no sign of humans. Hopefully the fishing would still be good this week-end.

The side passenger door opened and broke his thought pattern. Mary was standing in the pouring rain in her drenched rain suit staring at him with critical eyes and he could tell she was not in a good mood.

"The rain seems to be slowing down." she rasped with a hint of sarcasm and pulled herself up into the front seat. Her two companions looking like a pair of soaked cats climbed into the back and the truck began to move down the swampy tote road that had in years past been used for hauling logs to some loading site.

"Not far now," gurgled John, "The road ends down by the lake, but we'll park up above as it's too muddy down below, and we'll get stuck for sure."

In a few minutes he brought the truck to a stop and they all exited and began to untie the ropes holding the canoes while the ladies held the flashlights giving them some light. The forest now was in darkness and they could dimly see the lake through the trees a short distance away.

Mary pulled the tarp away uncovering the pack sacks in the box of the pick-up and began unloading them. The rain had subsided but the trees were dripping with moisture and the air hung heavy from the all day precipitation. The men finally unloaded the canoe and pulled on their packs and prepared to find their way to the lake. Slowly the group moved forward with the women in front trying to show the way with their flashlights. The two weak beams cast long slivers of light on the mud filled road that was strewn with rotting logs and fallen trees.

Some time later they arrived on the shore after a number of slips and stumbles in the dark and dropped the canoes and packs on the wet ground.

"Which way is the campsite?" Linda asked looking out over the dark lake. The rain was beginning to come down harder. John pointed to a distant point of land barely visible and asked, "How are you guys doing?"

"We're fine." she replied as water dripped from the end of her nose.

"Let's get these canoes loaded and get to the campsite." Rob was busy sliding the canoes out to the waters edge.

Once the canoes were loaded the friends began their voyage across the dark expanse of water while the rain continued to beat down. John and Mary took the lead and their companions stayed close behind. No one spoke and only the sound of rain and the blurp of the paddles could be heard in the night.

The point of land they were heading for seemed close at times and then far away. John wondered how their two friends were handling this difficult experience. He marveled that he had not heard a word of complaint or any whining which would be expected from many who came from a comfortable urban setting.

At last they came to land and slid their canoes up on a small sandy beach with a few large trees set behind. Mary leaned forward and stepped out unto the sand peering into the dark foliage looking for a clearing.

"Where"s the campsite?" she asked as she pulled the canoe further up so her husband could disembark.

Rob and Linda pulled up beside them relieved to have finally arrived at a spot they could set up their tents.

"There's a small clearing under those two big white pines a few feet ahead of you." John pointed a wet finger and then hauled out the packs from the canoe. Mary shone her flashlight through the trees and could vaguely see a small area barely large enough for one tent.

"Is that the spot you mean?" she asked, incredulous that this was the chosen site. She was tired and irritated. "How do you plan to set up our tents here?"

They were all chilled and tired and looked forward to a warm dry spot to sleep. They searched in the darkness for level ground that would be free from obstacles or bumps but instead found several enormous roots from two white pines that stretched far out across the small opening.

"Guess we'll go ahead and set up here." Rob mumbled as he pulled out his tent with damp cold fingers. The site was on a small hill that would constitute a challenge to keep from rolling sideways in the sleeping bags. The ground was soggy and uneven as they attempted to stake down the floor. John and Mary were close by fumbling with their tent and trying to piece together the aluminum poles using the small beam of light from the flashlight. The tents would be soaked as well as the rest of the gear by the time they were done.

"Wow, isn't this a lot of fun." Mary muttered, clearly exasperated.

Twenty minutes later the drenched tents were erected and the flys placed over them. Water was running under and around the outer edges as the rain continued to come down. They hoped the plastic bags that held the sleeping bags had kept them dry as well as their extra clothing.

Rob climbed into his tent and began blowing air into the damp mattresses. He felt chilled as his rain jacket had wet through and he longed to get inside his warm dry bag.

Linda's voice came to him from the tent opening, "My feet got wet even with these rubber boots on." Her husband did not respond but continued to blow air into the mattress.

In the other tent John had settled in for the night and was squirming around trying to find a spot that wasn't filled with humps or sharp points. The thin foam pad he was laying on did little to make life more comfortable from the raised tree root directly under him.

"My sleeping bag is soaked." Mary grumbled.

A soft voice from their friends tent was heard, "A night to remember." And then silence.

John had rolled over facing the tent wall when a cold drop of water landed on his forehead. He grunted and ran his hand on the tent floor near his face. A small stream of water was running past him and heading for the foam pad. The corner of the tent had sprung a leak.

Some time later he slipped into a fatigue induced sleep with visions of lying in a trench filled with cold water and raindrops hitting him in the face.

Mary lay beside him wide awake and shivering even though she had left her clothes on in the sleeping bag. She tried to sleep but felt miserable and upset. What ever had possessed her to come on this trip? Something underneath her was grinding into her hip and she moved sideways only to encounter a larger root. The sound of the rain on the tent roof had begun to calm her and then slowly she slipped into a state of semi consciousness.

Rob awoke and rubbed his eyes. Morning had arrived and the inside of the tent was bright from the sunlight filtering through the trees limbs. Crawling to the front of the tent he unzipped the door and looked out. The wet grass glistened in the sun and huge raindrops clung valiantly to the leaves above.

"Good morning John." he croaked as he made his way out of the tent.

"And to you as well, my man, did you sleep at all last night?" his friend asked, as he lit a match and placed it close to a burner of the small propane stove they would use for cooking.

"Yes, but it was a little damp and a little bumpy." came the reply.

"We'll have hot coffee as soon as it perks." The burner had given a big poof and ignited.

Linda and Mary both emerged from the rain drenched tents and stood looking about.

"No wonder I kept sliding off my mattress all night, we were on quite a slant." Linda remarked.

"Not to mention wet sleeping bags and big roots in the back." Mary added looking directly at her husband.

"That was a little rough, but the good news is that the sun is shining and it's going to be a great day." he said over his shoulder while sorting out the food items from his pack they would use for breakfast.

The sun was warm as it filtered through the sparse shrubs along the side of the clearing. Pine needles carpeted the area from two massive white pines that loomed above them. The lake a few short feet away had a glass like surface. The sky was clear and blue.

John felt good and gave thanks for the change in weather. The others were stomping around in an attempt to warm up while they ate their toast and drank hot coffee.

A pesky whiskey jack sat perched on a nearby limb looking for a handout. Rob laid a few pieces of bread on a rock and watched the friendly bird swoop down and land, without any evident nervousness. The bird made itself at home and began pecking away at the crumbs.

Mary went down to the beach and made herself comfortable on the front seat of the canoe letting the sun dry her clothes. She was beginning to feel better already from the hot coffee and toast and the warmth of the sun.

Rob and Linda soon arrived and pushed their canoe off the beach and paddled out from shore. The bright blue water shimmered in the sunlight as a small trout rose for a fly. As they slowed to a stop they marveled at the scene as the beauty of the north woods began to cast its timeless spell over them. They dropped their lures in the water and began to troll in hopes of catching a fish for supper.

Sometime later John was making his way to their canoe when Mary heard a loud hoot from across the water. Rob had hooked a fish and they watched as Lynda netted the colorful brook trout. This was a great way to start the day after a rough night. John shoved the canoe out from land and headed for a grove of dark green cedars that rimmed the edge of the nearest bay.

Mary cast an old yellow spinner far under an overhanging limb near shore. As she began her retrieve a large fish solidly struck the lure spraying water and thrashing from side to side. She reeled it in close to the side of the canoe and John slipped the net under and swung the brilliantly coloured trout into the centre of the craft.

On the far shoreline their friends had been trolling slowly along when Linda pointed to a tall dead spruce tree a few yards inland. "Look Rob at the big bird perched on top of that old tree."

"I believe it's an eagle," he replied excitedly. A majestic bald eagle sat viewing the lake from his lofty domain with little concern for the visitors below.

As he edged the canoe closer the large raptor watched, his body silhouetted against the clear blue sky. The canoe began to drift sideways from a gentle breeze and the large bird lifted and flew upwards above the tree tops. The white neck and tail feathers contrasted sharply with the dark brown of his body. He continued to fly higher and higher till he disappeared from sight.

The fishing was good as they used flashers and worm harnesses with several good sized trout being caught.

John moved their craft into a far bay where a mixture of balsams and birches crowded the shoreline flaunting their deep summer green. The surface of the lake rippled from the gentle paddle strokes as they edged around a jut of land.

"A moose, Hon! A moose!" Mary sang out and pointed ahead. A short fifty yards in front of them they could see a young cow swimming across the lake. The animals neck and head were extended well above the water with its huge ears standing straight up.

"Let's see if we can catch him?" John yelled as he dug his paddle deep in the water.

Mary turned in her seat to look at him. "Let's not." she

retorted.

The moose had spotted them and was headed for the nearest shore. John paddled furiously in a vain attempt to close the distance but his wife had no intention of helping. They were close enough to see the wild eyes of the animal looking back at them in fear and the sight and smell of the humans caused it to swim even harder.

As they approached the shoreline the massive brown body began rising out of the water, and the moose climbed up on the bank and shook itself. With one last look at the strangers he trotted back into the dark brush and disappeared from sight.

The two fishermen decided to head back to camp and clean their fish and have lunch. Far across the lake they barely could make out their chums seated on a large boulder far above the water.

Rob and Linda felt comfortable, relaxing in the sun watching the other canoe angling for the campsite. "Perhaps we should go soon." he commented with a small twinge of reluctance in his voice. It was seldom he had enjoyed this much peace and solitude.

"Sure nice here but lunch will taste good." replied Linda. "We should have a nap and pack up if we plan to go home to-day."

Evening had arrived and the four tired campers tied on the two canoes on top of the green truck. Their energy had decreased through the day from being in the sun and fresh air. They had decided to head home as the forecast was rain the following day and they all felt it would be good to have a hot shower and lay in a soft bed.

John jumped in the front seat and turned the key. A muffled roar came from beneath the hood. He was thankful the machine had started as it was thirty miles to the nearest town and there would likely be no one back here to help out if the truck did not go. The old engine didn't sound quite right and thought he detected a knock in the engine.

The rest piled in and they soon were heading back down the tote road and making their way over the polished granite rock. John knew it would be dusk by the time they arrived at the little hamlet many miles away.

The road was extremely rough with all the pot holes and ruts causing them to drive very slowly. Once on the way the four began to reminisce about all that had happened on the trip. As they rattled along and endured the bumps they joked and laughed about the hardships of the night before. All seemed like a dream now, the paddle across the lake in the rain in the dark, setting up the tents using only small flashlights, sleeping on the big bumpy roots all night. It all seemed so long ago after the great day of sunshine and fishing.

"Clank, Bang!"

"What was that?" came a fearful voice from the backseat.

"I'm not sure." John responded, but he knew the sound had come from under the hood. "It didn't sound good."

"Oh great," Mary thought to herself, "Here we are miles in the bush and we're going to break down."

A distinct clanking noise could now be heard as the truck slowed.

"Do you think we are going to make it out?" Rob asked with a tint of concern in his voice. He felt bushed but he was a man who rarely fretted and would prepare himself for any outcome. His trust lay in a relationship with his Lord Jesus Christ as did the others in the truck.

"Let's hope so." his friend whispered but kept his foot on the gas petal afraid the engine would stall. He knew they had little chance of making it out if a piston had blown as he suspected and they would need to set up camp in the dark along the side of the road.

Slowly they proceeded along the isolated logging road, painfully eking out a mile at a time as the truck had lost most of its power.

Inside the cab everyone sat quiet, the laughter and joking had ceased. The hope they would make it to the small town filled their thoughts. No one wished to spend the night on the side of the road and then the next day hope that someone would come along to give them a ride.

The old engine continued to groan and grate as it chugged along. Gradually they could feel the truck lose power but as the miles dropped away their hopes increased. Then a strong odor of oil began to find its way into the cab.

Each one was silently praying the old vehicle would keep going. John knew it would be a miracle but God had brought him out of stressful situations before.

Mile after mile went by and suddenly they could see the long line of jack pines that welcomed them to the little village of Searchmont. A great sigh of relief filled the cab as they pulled the worn out Dodge into the driveway of their friend Flo. The truck lurched to a stand still and stalled. John turned the key and tried to restart it. There was one last loud bang and the engine died forever. They stepped out of the truck and met Flo who had come from his house to see what the noise was all about.

After a short explanation of the trip out they thanked God for answering their prayer.

"This has been a most memorable trip." remarked Linda smiling faintly.

"I'll take you back to town folks, and you can tell me the rest of the story on the way." Flo said and headed for his car. "And I can tell you now that this indeed is the end of the road for that old Dodge."

The End

Written by John Gearey

A Short Bear Story

The following story is a tale of two men and a bear. I believe it bears telling (if you can forgive the pun) as there may be something we can learn from it especially if you are a hiker or outdoors man.

On a certain morning in June my wife and I were at our camp and our friend Cris had arrived the day before to hook up the new propane fridge and stove he had brought with him. The job was finished and he was preparing to leave when the thought came to me that a walk back from Moose Lake would be refreshing. I had always enjoyed hiking and had found it to be a good way to get a little exercise.

Walking accelerates the heart beat, strengthens the leg muscles and fills the lungs with fresh air. I had been in the practice of taking daily walks in the past but the time of the year was June and for those who have not sallied forth during this wonderful time of the year in the outdoors of northern Canada need to experience it to appreciate it. And now was the first week of the heaviest hatch of the little blood sucking bugs we call black flies and mosquitoes. They wait patiently by the thousands to pounce on any red blooded hiker that dares to take a walk in the outback. Because of these aforementioned little devils I had not been out for a walk for sometime and felt that I needed to take a stroll to stretch the legs and get the heart pumping.

The morning had arrived bright and clear. One of those mornings when one feels alive and old hikers find themselves strapping on their hiking boots and heading down the nearest trail without fully understanding all the complexities of the moment.

Cris and I were in the backyard of the camp loading up his half ton for the trip home. The sun felt warm on the face. A slight breeze ruffled the new green leaves on the white birches that surrounded the cabin. I had caught the fever.

"Cris" I yelled out to my chum, "Can I catch a ride over to Moose Lake. "I'll walk back and get some exercise."

"Are you sure you want to do that?" Cris replied with a question that seemed to have some concern in it. "There's a lot of bear around this year and you told me last night you have no bear spray."

I thought about that for a moment. It was true there had been several bear sightings in the nearest town but that was fifty miles away. Then I remembered a story a logger had told me of a close encounter he had with a black bear only a week ago.

He had been in his camper on the job site and had gone to bed for the night when he heard a knock on the outside wall. As he rolled out of bed he wondered who would be visiting at that time of night when he heard a sound similar to that of ripping metal. Grabbing his flashlight he slowly opened the camper door and stepped outside. Shining the light around the clearing and along the side of the trailer he spotted a good sized black bear standing on a piece of aluminum siding it had torn off the trailer a few minutes earlier. The man yelled at the animal while waving the flashlight and the bear ran towards the nearest tree and began to climb it. But half way up it changed its mind and came back down and started coming towards the logger. All his waving and yelling didn't seem to scare the bear as it came closer and closer. Finally in desperation the fellow ran to a large tree farmer (a machine on wheels that moves trees) that stood nearby and climbed up into it. Starting the machine up he turned on all the lights and honked the horn. The bear was by now very close but seemed unaffected by the noise of the engine or the horn. It did not want to leave. The man put the big machine into a forward motion and started for the bear. The animal finally turned and ambled slowly off into the bush.

Thus my thoughts were about bears that do not scare and remembrances of other stories of bear attacks in Ontario that had been tragic. Should I be concerned and take the advise of my friend and not risk meeting a bear on the trail.

"Naw, I'll be fine Cris, I haven't seen a bear on the back road in all the years we've been coming here." I replied, hoping he wouldn't detect the shade of apprehension in my voice.

Without any more being said we climbed into the cab of Cris's green half ton and started down the bumpy road. The trees and bush that lined the road had formed a dark green canopy overhead and made it feel as if we were driving through a dimly lit tunnel.

Moose Lake lay only a short mile from the cabin, hidden in a valley a few yards off the road. The stream that ran through our property had its origins from this small lake that sat high on the hill behind the camp. As we drove slowly along I told Cris how only a week ago I'd crept to the edge of the precipice that overlooked the lake and scanned the far shoreline in hopes of seeing a moose. All I could see were a pair of mallards paddling around in the centre. As I turned to head back to the main road something caught my eye.

Directly below me in six feet of water stood a large cow moose. The creatures' ears stood erect and with big wide eyes it was staring up at me without moving. What a sight! The memory and the thrill of seeing this giant animal submerged in the water was still vivid.

Cris brought the truck to an abrupt stop on top of the hill close to the trail that led to the lake.

"Thanks Cris for the ride and have a safe trip home." I blurped as I jumped down from the truck.

"You to John." he responded with a strange look in his eyes.

I stood watching the rear end of the flat bed truck disappear around the corner before I strolled quietly in to take a look at Moose Lake. Perhaps the moose I had seen earlier would still be hanging around or taking a dip to get away from the flies.

The sun sparkled on the surface of the water with tiny brilliant lights bouncing high in the air. Along the shallow shoreline was an abundance of lily pads and water cresses that made excellent fodder for the moose. However on this day there was no moose in sight.

I headed to the main road and began the hike home. With long swift strides I knew that it would not take long to make it back to camp, but as I walked I began to recall what my friend had said about the bears and their unusual aggressive behavior lately towards humans. I began to recall a documentary I'd seen on T.V. recently about black bears, and what to do if you happen to meet up with one.

To begin with the expert had said to make a lot of noise when hiking in bear country so as not to walk on them unexpectedly and startle them.

Good idea I thought so I began to sing out the first thing that came to mind. Now I must say that I was never endowed with the gift of singing but out here who was to hear me. Furthermore it was evident my mind had become over concerned with the prospect of meeting a bear and the possible consequences of such an encounter. But as I had told Cris I had never seen a bear on this road and I had been up and down it a hundred times. What was there to worry about.

However I began to sing out in my loudest voice just in case.

"I hope I see a bear, Ho, ho, I hope I see a bear!" and I kept rapping it out as I moved along.

What would ever make a sane man sing those words I will never know. The day was great for hiking and I felt good. Who cared what I sounded like, any bear hearing that noise would high tail as fast as he could.

"I hope I see a bear, ho, ho!" I roared out as I rounded the corner of the old logging road. I skidded to an abrupt halt. My heart jumped in my throat. There standing a short hundred feet away in the middle of the road was the biggest black bear I had ever seen and I had seen a lot of bear over the years.

"Oh no!" I breathed out loud with my heart pumping far too

fast. "I didn't mean it Lord, I was only kidding." I tried to stay calm and not panic.

I had seen many black bears in the bush during the past forty years but this one appeared different. For one thing this big fellow didn't run away like most bears do when crossing paths with humans. Was this the breed of bear that we'd been hearing about that had no fear of mankind like the one the logger had encountered at the campsite? Obviously my awful singing and yelling hadn't worried the bear in the least. So much for the experts and their advice. I wondered what would happen now.

The big bear simply stood its ground and watched me intently. Neither of us made a move in the first few seconds but my mind was groping for an answer of what to do and my body was screaming run you idiot! Then I began to recall what the documentary had recommended if you did come face to face with a bear. First don't try to run away. Bears take that as a sign of fear and will chase you and catch you very quickly. As well, do not try to play dead as black bear attacks are usually fatal. Unlike the grizzly they will continue to maul you and even eat you if hungry. Something I didn't care to think about right now. The program suggested to start jumping up and down, waving your arms wildly making yourself appear larger. Should the bear begin to come towards you, pick up rocks and throw them at it. Never show fear and fight for your life.

Well that all sounded fine and good when I was at home safe in front of a television set but out here in front of a huge beast that seemed to be licking its chops and eying me up and down I wondered if I had the courage. I looked quickly around for a rock to throw. Not a rock in sight. Not good.

The bear was still standing in the same spot not moving. I wondered what he was thinking.

These big boars can be aggressive and mean I had heard.

"Oh well, here's goes nothing," I muttered to myself as my fear level rose. I began jumping in the air, waving my arms frantically, and yelling at the top of my voice.

"Go on, get outa here, go on!"

The bear watched me for a few seconds as I jumped up and down and then turned slowly towards me. He gave me a long look of disdain. It was evident that this bear was no more afraid of me than some little ant in his path. The feeling of alarm was spreading through my innards. I wished I had one of those so called experts beside me right now.

I carried on with my antics screaming at the big animal and waving my arms wildly.

"Go on, get going, go on!"

Suddenly he pivoted on his back legs and taking one long last look at me disappeared into the brush along the side of the road.

"Whew! That was a close one." I mumbled under my breath while giving thanks, but what now. I hesitated and watched the side of the road ahead of me where the bear had just entered.

I had to walk down the road past the spot where "Ben" had gone in the bush.

The thought was uppermost in my mind that he could be waiting inside the thick foliage and still be considering what he would do with me.

Gathering all the courage I could muster I headed down the road at a brisk pace. Eyeballing the edge of the road I walked past the spot where the bear had entered only minutes before.

"Great! So far so good." I thought as I booted up the next rise on the road. However I knew from experience that bears can often circle a target and reappear suddenly ahead of it. And they can move through the brush with hardly a sound.

I tried to not think of these things or allow those thoughts to overwhelm me, so I slowed down. Yes I suppose old Mr. Bruin might show up at any moment ahead of me or even behind me but I had seen no movement or heard any sound for the last few minutes. I knew I must stay calm.

I reasoned that if he was hungry I would have been bear supper already so I continued to walk forward up the next hill and around a bend in the road while occasionally taking a glimpse behind me.

In all my years of hiking in the bush I had never been very concerned about being around wildlife or the safety issues. Now for the first time a wake up call on reality and it made me feel a touch uncomfortable. No one wants to admit they can be afraid at some point.

In a few minutes I reached the cabin and began to tell my wife of the little episode over a glass of cold ice tea. As I took a long slow drink I knew deep in my heart I would never be quite the same carefree hiker I'd been in the past.

"Where did you say we could buy some of that bear spray honey?" I asked.

In closing I wish to ask my dear readers if they can detect a moral to this story? Perhaps even two.

Do you remember the concern of my friend before my hike. Always consider the words of a friend. And do you remember my song of asking to see a bear? Never ask for something you don't really want, because I believe God has a sense of humor and you just might get what you ask for!

The end.

Written by John Gearey

Ira

Remembering Ira

The following story is about a young man and his friend Ira who was seventy years old at the time they took one of several trips into the wilderness in search of the elusive speckled trout. We may never really understand the mind set of an older man who would walk miles in the heat and bugs in the bush exhausting his body to the limit but I hope the tale to follow will be viewed as a tribute from his young friend who now finds himself in the senior time of life. I hope this small adventure will not only intrigue you but give you an appreciation of the quality and stamina of the man called Ira.

The day was warm as two men trudged along a gravel logging road that wound its way deep into Lake Superior Park. The road no longer accessible to motorized vehicles had become a route used by hikers and fishermen. John a man in his early thirties and his older chum Ira were hoping to fulfill Ira's dream of fishing fabled Woodpecker Lake before he grew too old to handle the trek.

"Man alive it's hot already and it's only ten o'clock." John declared wiping his forehead with the sleeve of his shirt.

"Yes I'm still alive," Ira replied with his usual dry wit. His surname was Mann. "But if we have to climb many more of these hills I won't be."

John cracked a smile and kept walking but he had to agree the hills were steep and the packs too heavy for this long a carry.

Ira's backpack had an external frame and had been loaded with meticulous care. Each item had been thoughtfully assessed for usefulness before it was put in. He was a master at packing all kinds of goodies into the sack when hiking with his young friend to lakes he had only hoped to fish till now.

After a slow arduous climb they finally made it to the top of their fourth steep hill. John came to a stop and slowly slid his interior frame pack off his shoulders and collapsed on the ground beside it.

Ira walked up to a big boulder on the side of the road and sat down against it. "I'll leave my sack on, it's too heavy to put back on." he stated as he took out a small canteen of water and slurped back some of the contents.

John looked thoughtfully at his older friend. The day was going to be hot and dry but the hot sun would help keep the mosquitoes and black flies away.

"How are you doing so far?" he asked.

"I'll let you know when we get there." Ira replied with his usual dead pan look. After a short rest John stood and took a long swig from his water bottle. Ira helped him lift his pack on his back and they headed down the road without a word.

A short time later they could see Mash Lake through the trees. It was the first of a chain of lakes that an old skid road wound around and would bring them closer to their destination. They slipped off the gravel road down unto an overgrown path and were soon forced to move slowly through a maize of tag alders and small evergreens.

John was becoming concerned of Ira's stamina as they battled their way through the tightly woven bushes. He had convinced his friend he could handle the walk in but as the sun beat down and with only a slight breeze to refresh them he began to have some doubts.

Midday arrived as the two hikers made their way past Lost Lake. John felt better now as the abandoned tote road had become wider with fewer trees making the walking easier. The Wire

Houser map showed the trail avoiding Found Lake and curling its way around Corner and Snipe Lake where it dead ended. The trail was wet and boggy, with mud filling the deep ruts made long ago by the great skidders used in pulling out the logs. Quack grass grew high along the furrows causing the men to slip and slide on the obscure edges.

Ira kept pushing forward without complaining which amazed his younger friend. How well he managed the rough terrain at his age was a tribute to how much he loved exploring the wilderness and going fishing.

"There's Corner Lake." John pointed through the dense brush towards a glint of blue water. He paused for a moment of rest and listened to the wind as it passed through the tops of the tall white pines near the lake.

Ira arrived behind him and immediately sat down on an old decayed stump that was draped in a green brackish moss.

"Does this trail come closer to Corner Lake?" Ira asked wearily.

"No. In fact from here on it swings away and becomes a rough path to an unnamed lake south of here." John replied.

"How much further to Woodpecker do you think it is? questioned Ira as he stared off into the distance as if looking for a sign in the sky.

"See that hill ahead of us? John waved in the general direction of a very large and high hill. "We have to make it over that hill to get to the lake."

Ira bowed his head and looked intently at the pale yellow mounds of grass that grew at his feet. His faded blue eyes had sunk far back in his head and his face had turned a strange color of gray.

"I don't think I have the strength to go any further." he blurted out.

John turned and looked at the man whom he had so convincingly enticed to come on this long difficult hike. "You don't feel well?" he asked his friend.

Ira didn't respond but continued to stare at the ground. Deep emotions were welling up inside and he was far from being an emotional man. His mind said keep going but his body was saying don't move. Here he was after all the planning and preparation sitting on a stump sweating and exhausted knowing they still had two miles of bush and a steep hill to get over. How could he ever do it? And yet deep down he really wanted to make it and not let his friend down and spoil the trip. He remained sitting on the stump in deep contemplation without saying a word.

John had been watching Ira closely not knowing what the best course of action should be. On one hand there was too much swamp and brush to make it to Corner Lake and no campsite to set up in and no canoe to get them across the lake to the one on the opposite shore.

To attempt to set up camp here in the wet marsh with no fresh water would be a last resort. However on the other hand if they continued on with the old lad in this condition he might collapse from exhaustion and possibly even die.

Time was moving on and a decision had to be made and soon.

"Do you want to try to go a little further Ira?" John asked hoping the short rest had given his friend some extra energy.

Ira nodded his head ever so slightly and mumbled something unintelligible and looked at his packsack. "I need a shot of scotch." he grumbled.

John looked into Ira's eyes. "You can make it my friend. I know you can. Let's give it one more try."

The older man still looking haggard and beat slowly stood and took a deep breath. All his pride and desire filled his heart but he had made the decision to keep going. John helped him slip his pack over his tired and sore shoulders.

"Let's go." he grunted and watched his partner take the lead. Should he collapse in the bush John would have to haul him out one way or another.

The younger man moved forward with a gnawing feeling of guilt that he should have more compassion for others especially when they were hurting. He was still young and strong and eagerly wished to find the lake to-day without taking into account the well being of his old friend.

The road narrowed and then ended in a tangled mess of alders. John charged forward with one hand separating the dense brush and the other trying to protect his face from the small sharp branches. Suddenly and without warning he tripped over a hidden log and fell face first into a mass of wild raspberry bushes bruising his shin and scratching his face. Rolling over on his back he rubbed his throbbing leg.

"You okay?" Ira commented in his usual dry voice with no sign of emotion. "Great place to brake a leg."

"Yeah, but a few more yards and we'll start up the hill and be in the hardwoods and the walking will be a lot easier." John replied as he rolled over on his knees and hoisted himself to his feet. He readjusted his pack and viewed the hill ahead. The climb would be taxing and he only could hope his chum would have the endurance to make it to the top.

Both men were soon gasping for air as they progressed up the steep hillside pausing frequently to catch their breath. There had been no communication for some time as the climb was taking all the strength they could muster. John had become like a man possessed as he pushed on without much consideration of his partner. He seemed obsessed with reaching the top so they could at least see the lake and start down the hill towards it. He wondered briefly why he was not more considerate and kind? The thought crossed his mind how he would ever be able to explain to Ira's wife why her husband didn't come back especially since he told her he would take care of him? Of course it was his fault. He could have stopped and set up an emergency camp and given his chum time to recover. But no as usual he had to push to the limit.

He looked back and yelled "You're almost at the top, Ira."

The afternoon sun had slipped behind a hill as they came to level ground and began to work their way across the top. John felt tired and could only imagine how his companion felt who was double his age. They needed to be cautious as they began their descent on the back half of the hill. He knew that the day's exhaustive trip would have weakened their legs and the extra weight on their backs could send them crashing forward too quickly and cause a serious injury.

The two bushwhackers stopped for a moment half way down and viewed the distant lake known as Woodpecker. Ira seemed to be a little stronger and John felt better now that they could see their goal. However Ira still looked pale and exhausted and John felt a moment of sympathy sweep over him.

"O Lord, give the man the strength to make it to the lake and be able to go fishing."

A few more minutes of descent found them crossing over an old skid road and pushing down through the alders and out unto a cluster of rocks on the edge of the lake. At last they had arrived. Ira leaned on a paddle and looked out over the tranquil water. His dream had come to pass.

John had left an old canoe hidden safely out of sight a year ago and hoped he could find it without it being cracked or broken. He began his search near a large spruce tree with low overhanging branches a hundred feet down the lake. Within minutes he espied what appeared to be the end of the canoe. Throwing the brush and evergreen limbs off he found no major cracks from the weight of the winter snow. Thankful that no one had found it in the fall he pulled it out to the waters edge and went back to retrieve his packsack. Ira came slowly forward with a look of relief.

"Come on John, let's get moving."

Long slender shadows sliced across the dark blue water as they pushed off shore and began to paddle towards the campsite at the end of the lake. Neither man spoke a word as they relaxed in deep thought.

John's eyes popped open as the smell of bacon and coffee invaded the tent in the early hours of the following morning. Ira as usual had risen first, started the fire and had the coffee brewing. John felt relieved. The older man had recovered from yesterdays long trek and was out by the fire frying bacon waiting patiently for his young friend to climb out of the sack.

"Good morning Ira, how do you feel this morning?" a voice from inside the tent peeled out through the crisp air.

"Lousy," came the reply."

"Ready to go for some trout?"

"That's what we're here for." grunted Ira.

John appeared by the fire and looked at his companion. He didn't seem any the worse for wear and appeared ready for a day's fishing. They had planned on two days of traveling and three days of fishing. John hoped the day out would be cooler and no rain, but that was a long time in the future.

"Well Ira, no rain and the bugs could be worst for the first of June. I'll cook us some eggs seeing you have the bacon going." He went over to a nearby spruce tree where he had hung his packsack the night before. Unzipping it he brought out a mug, plate, fork and four eggs wrapped in a newspaper in a can. Pleased they were intact he strolled over to the fire and stole some bacon grease from Ira's pan, broke open the eggs and placed them in the spare skillet he had.

After breakfast the pair cleaned up and prepared their gear to go fishing. Ira was always very careful and kept everything in order. He always cut extra wood for the fire, the utensils and plates polished and the campsite spotless. John had great respect for this gentleman who was always willing to go on fishing trips, especially trips to more remote lakes.

They loaded their canoe and pushed off shore with Ira in the bow his small box of lures between his feet. He wore a life jacket most of the time as he had never learned to swim even though once when he was young he had ended up in the cold spring waters of a lake after the boat he was in capsized. Fortunately his partner and he were rescued in the nick of time before succumbing to the numbing cold water and with no life jacket on he had been forced to cling to the side of the boat till he was rescued.

"What are using for tackle." asked Ira nonchalantly a question often heard from one fishermen to another regardless of age or experience.

"The usual flasher with a trailer and a worm." came the reply. "Let's hope they're biting." He crushed a mosquito on the back of his neck.

"Well it doesn't matter what I use. I'm always bad luck for everyone, you'll see." muttered Ira.

As the morning progressed John caught four good sized brook trout that had fought gallantly and Ira with great skill netted each one. He had missed netted fish over the years and no one seemed to take kindly to it. He never could understand why some thought it so important to land every fish they hooked. There were lots more of them in the lake.

Although his chum had faithfully netted each fish he could tell Ira was growing discouraged by the look creeping over his grey countenance. The fisherman had not had a strike all morning while his partner had been having many hits.

"Try this set up I've been using Ira." John said and handed over a rig similar to the one he'd been using.

"Alright, but I know it's not the lure it's me. I have no luck." came the response.

The sun was now high in the sky and the wind had begun to blow briskly. John was seated in the stern and did most of the paddling. Ira was seated facing him and was the way they usually fished which allowed the older man to stay in the canoe for longer periods of time without cramping up.

Two hours passed and John was growing weary from paddling up against the brisk wind but Ira didn't seem to notice. His eyes had taken on a peculiar glint. The fortunes of fishing had changed and now five large beautiful trout were on his stringer.

The day for him had turned around as gloom had turned to joy but not for his friend who was paddling furiously against the wind and had not caught another fish. The fickleness of the elusive speckled trout. Why he wondered when both of them were using identical rigs.

"Let's go ashore and have lunch." spouted John

"Sounds good to me," Ira replied. They had been in the canoe for four hours with only one short break and his legs had stiffened considerably.

Lunch for Ira consisted of crackers and cheese and a can of sardines along with hot tea. The tea was boiled in a used tomato can and hung by a wire on a wooden stick above the fire. He always shared little snacks from the hidden recesses of his pack and could include any number of things from cookies to candies. John had pulled out a container with sliced bread and slapped on some peanut butter and washed it down with gator-aid.

After their snack the pair retired to the tent for an afternoon nap. Later they would try casting along the shoreline before having a delicious supper of fried trout, rice and beans and enjoy the evening fire. The days of fishing all day were long past and their bodies needed to recover from the exertion that had been expended the day before.

The following two days were days of good fishing with warm, sunny weather. On the last day two unusual things happened. While they were busy casting to shore one morning trying different types of lures ranging from Mepps to Cleo's and other hardware a distinct whacking sound reverberated in the area of the canoe. John felt pain as Ira's blue and silver Cleo bounced off the side of his head and fell beside him. He looked at his friend who had a look of disbelief on his face. A close call as the treble hooks had not caught an ear or eye which would have made for a difficult situation.

Ira was grasping for words to apologize as he was usually so very careful in whatever he did. "Sorry John, I don't know what happened."

"That's okay. I needed to wake up anyhow."

After a good morning of catching fish the two ate lunch and retired for a short spell in the afternoon. Ira fell asleep immediately but John laid back on his sleeping bag and listened to the deep guttural snore coming from next to him. The tent was warm from the sun and a slight breeze ruffled the door flaps and his eyelids closed as he passed into dream world.

John awoke with a start. He had heard a noise close by outside the tent. The first thought was a bear. The sound came from near the firepit and was definitely a wild animal scrounging around. If it was a bear they had a big problem. It would be nice to have a pistol but that was illegal in Canada. He leaned forward and peered out through the screening of the door. A sigh of relief spread over him as he recognized what the varmint was. Instead of a big black bear he could see a large brown groundhog poking around the edge of the pit. The animal had to be one of the largest he had ever seen. As a teenager one of his pastimes was shooting groundhogs and he had seen some really big ones. The rodents dug holes all over the hay fields and multiplied like crazy so the owners hired him to cut down on the quantity of the little varmints.

The little devil in him welled up as the old days came back and he envisioned putting a bullet between the eyes of the harmless creature. Now that would be a fine thing. Given the opportunity he might succumb to the temptation and not only kill the poor thing but most likely scare the living daylights out of his sleeping friend, maybe even give him a heart attack. His thoughts came back to reality and he was simply thankful that it was a groundhog and not a hungry bear.

The days had flown by and the two friends had fished and canoed the whole lake but finally the day to depart arrived. Ira and his young friend repacked their sacks in the early morning and eat breakfast. They now sat on two well aged logs reminiscing of other trips. Ira was in a good mood and unusually talkative. He claimed it was the best trip he'd ever been on but he sure didn't look forward to the trip out. Giving John some left over goodies which made his pack lighter he tied up the front securely. The plan was for him to carry the two paddles, fishing rods and the bag of fourteen big trout as well as the pack on his back. Meanwhile John would carry the short canoe over the big hill down to Snipe Lake and then paddle the two lakes Corner and Snipe and finally portage up to the unused logging road hoping to carry the canoe the next five miles to their vehicle.

The sun was already thrusting yellow shafts of light through the surrounding trees as the forest came alive. They hurriedly finished their clean-up of the camp and loaded the canoe for the trip down the lake. White throated sparrows sang out their melody as if in farewell to their visitors.

The two men found a spot to land near where they had embarked only a few days earlier and in a short time were ready to head up through the hardwoods on the side of the hill separating Woodpecker and Snipe Lake. John was already plunging across the tote road with the canoe balanced on his shoulders and his sack swinging on his back. Ira was loaded down with his pack and another small sack strapped around his neck while hanging unto the paddles, net and the bag of fish. Had there been any witnesses they might have assumed this burdened down pair of bushwhackers would never make it over the big hill.

Ira had come to the overgrown tote road that John had recently crossed. He could see his chum beginning his climb up through the hardwoods.

"Hold up John, I'm taking this old road as I'm sure it skirts the hill and it may work it's way over to the no name lake. I am not going to climb that hill you're on."

"That road doesn't go anywhere Ira." John yelled back to his friend. He had studied the maps and had seen no road of any kind. "Follow me Ira, we'll take our time."

Ira didn't reply and was already trying to follow a dim trail that indeed seemed to be heading around the base of the hill. John simply shrugged and continued weaving in and out of the maples and yellow birches that covered the steep ridge. As he climbed higher he began breathing deeper and the weight of the canoe and pack caused him to stagger occasionally with his heart pumping wildly screaming for more oxygen.

Stopping at the mid point he scanned the side of the hill but was unable to see through the deep brush at the bottom or hear any sound of his chum. Plodding upwards John had determined to make the crest as quickly as possible. Pausing several times he listened but heard no sound from below. Where was that old guy he wondered? Maybe he had found some old trail and was far away by now. They should have stayed together and not struck off separately. Both these men were stubborn at times or better said head strong. The leaves of the trees and brush were thick now with the new spring growth making visibility difficult.

"Ira, Ira, where are you?" John yelled at the top of his voice. He stood the canoe upright in the crotch of a small maple tree and dropped his packsack on the ground. He couldn't afford to let the equipment out of his sight knowing he might not find it again or at least have to search for hours to locate it. He stood and listened for some time but the forest was silent.

"Oh boy, here we go again, I guess I'll never learn." he muttered aloud as he remembered one time on the way out of Surf Lake his old chum had done almost the same thing by taking off on some supposed short cut. The younger man had propped his canoe up against a tree with his sack and headed in the general direction Ira had gone. Yelling at the top of his voice he continued searching for him for nearly an hour but could not locate him. Very discouraged he decided to head back to where he had left his canoe and sack and take them down to the landing on the next lake. And that was when the nightmare grew worse.

Traveling back through the bush in what he supposed was the correct route he soon found the trees and the area all seemed alike. Arriving in the spot where he was sure he had left the canoe he could find no sign of it. Somehow everything had disappeared in the lush green foliage of the woods. He would never forget the feelings that ran through him during that next half hour. Not only had he lost his chum who was more vulnerable than he but as well lost his equipment. Imagine trying to explain that to anyone.

Eventually Ira did show up at the next lake and John found his stuff but he had promised himself to never ever get in that situation again. And now here he was in the same situation once more yelling through the trees in hope of hearing Ira's voice. Once again he must go in search of the man.

"Ira, where are you?" John called loudly as he walked along the rim of the hill while keeping the canoe in sight. Still getting no answer or hearing any sound he continued to call out Ira's name. John's thoughts began to conjure up all kinds of things. What if he never found him. How would he explain this to Ira's wife Bea, Would he say something like "Oh he just wandered off on his own and I let him go." Now wouldn't that sound jimdandy. The truth being he'd gone and let the older man go by himself and he had stubbornly as usual kept right on trucking up the hill with only one purpose and that was to get to the top as quickly as possible. First he had pushed Ira far too hard going in and now he'd gone and lost him. Great going.

John gave his head a shake and tried to refocus. He knew he must find Ira one way or another.

Then through the clear morning air he was sure he heard a faint sound far away. "Where are you Ira?"

From far below amidst the tangled green growth came a barely distinguishable voice. "I'm down here on my hands and knees. I don't think I can get up this hill."

Ira was attempting to climb up the backside of the steep hill covered with dense brush while still dragging the paddles, rods and bag of fish. Relief washed over John. "Ira, I'm over this way. Keep coming."

After what seemed an eternity to John, Ira finally appeared through the maze of trees. He was on his feet but moving slowly

171

and totally exhausted. His face even grayer than usual with a worn wasted look. He looked all his seventy years. John felt sympathy for him but didn't know what to say.

"I've got to rest awhile." Ira gasped as he slumped down on a rock. "That skid road petered out so I started up this hill hoping to find you."

John was eager to keep moving but knew his friend needed time to recover. "I left the canoe on the crest of the ridge and when you're feeling up to it we'll head that way." he said and grabbed the bag of fish that must have weighed close to thirty pounds. The fish were in a double pillow case with maple leaves to keep them cool. As soon as they came to a lake they would dip the bag in the water and the vaporization would help preserve the trout.

Ira looked at the young man with a pained look and then stood up. The morning was quickly moving on and they had a long way to go.

The pair soon were slipping around the large hardwoods on the flat part of the ridge stepping carefully over the dead falls and rotting logs in their path. As they began to descend into a shallow valley John came to an abrupt stop. Rising from the floor of the depression rose a tall dead spruce completely void of any green. On the pinnacle of the stark grey spear of a tree was a red tanager, a bird seldom if ever seen this far north.

Excitedly John pointed at the bird silhouetted against the blue sky. "Look Ira at the beautiful bird!"

"Who cares about some bird." Ira grumbled and kept on the move wondering why anyone would take time to look at some dumb bird when he was almost dead from exhaustion.

Close to an hour later the two tired fishermen came to the shores of an unnamed lake that would lead them to the portage to Snipe Lake. After a short paddle they slid the canoe up unto the soft black mud that marked the trail. They soon were crashing through tightly woven saplings and scraggly raspberry bushes that tore at their clothing and bare hands. Ugly red welts began to appear on their exposed skin and Ira was softly muttering under his breath.

John was using the canoe as a battery ram to push forward between the legion of tag alders that stood in the way all the while hearing the screeching of the branches on the sides hoping they didn't do too much damage.

After the short difficult portage they came to a bay on Snipe Lake.

Both men were drained of all energy as they drank from their canteens and loaded their canoe for the trip up the lake.

The sun was warm as they paddled through the clear green water and let their bodies relax after the hard carry over the hill. Perhaps they would come to this lake again as they knew there were many trout still swimming wild waiting for someone to catch them. Ira relaxed in the bow and let his young friend paddle slowly through a small channel leading to Corner Lake. He watched an old campsite slip by and wished they could stop for awhile. Maybe some day he would come back here but he knew in his heart he would never see Woodpecker Lake again.

Further down the lake they entered a narrow dog leg of shallow water. Balsam and cedar trees lined the one side and maples and birches covered the hill opposite. Neither man seemed inclined to talk and seemed happy to paddle along deep in their own thoughts. Exhausted and tired they savored the rest time while mentally preparing for the five mile walk ahead of them.

A few minutes of paddling brought them to a clearing amongst a willow covered shoreline with tall grass and murky water. They pulled ashore and unloaded and prepared to follow a dim trail that led to the gravel road.

"Finally," rasped Ira, "We'll be out in three hours."

"We hope." mumbled John under his breath. He hoped Ira would be able to make it.

North of the Soo

Once up on the dusty road leading to the highway they seemed to have renewed strength and began to talk about the trip. Back at the landing John knew he did not have the strength to carry the canoe all the way out so would need to leave it in the bush. He would come back and carry it out as soon as he could. Hopefully no one came along and took it, but that was a risk he was willing to take.

As they began to trudge down the road John took the bag of fish from Ira.

"Thanks, my arms feel like they've been pulled out of their sockets."

John had taken note that his old friend never asked him to carry anything and except for the rough parts of the bush never complained. His estimation of the older man's strength had grown immensely. Few men could handle the rigorous terrain in the heat at his age.

By late afternoon the two hikers had arrived back at their vehicle. Both now were desperately tired as they prepared to drive the two hours back home. John hoped he wouldn't fall asleep at the wheel and Ira wondered if he would ever go on another trip with his friend. Well maybe once he recovered from this one.

The End

Written by John Gearey
March 2014

Other Books by Author John H.Gearey

1. North of the Soo
2. East of Superior
3. Destiny Unknown
4. Mystery on Crystal Lake

Note by Author. I have been asked if I plan to write a sequel to 'Destiny Unknown?' Yes, I am presently in the process of writing the sequel of the young couple in the James Bay Lowlands wilderness area. As well I am working on another book of short stories of people who have had amazing and life threatening events happen in their lives. Presently I have been interviewing pilots, train engineers and other outdoor folks.

Thank-you to all my readers.

I thank the firm O.J.Graphix Inc., Bill and John and the staff situated in the town of Espanola, Ontario for their work in re-printing the book 'North of the Soo' which is the 8th printing.

J.G.